TRACKING
AND READING SIGN

A Guide to Mastering the Original Forensic Science

Len McDougall

Skyhorse Publishing

Skyhorse Publishing books may be purchased in bulk at special discounts for sales promotion, corporate gifts, fund-raising, or educational purposes. Special editions can also be created to specifications. For details, contact the Special Sales Department, Skyhorse Publishing, 555 Eighth Avenue, Suite 903, New York, NY 10018 or info@skyhorsepublishing.com.

www.skyhorsepublishing.com

10 9 8 7 6 5 4 3 2 1

Library of Congress Cataloging-in-Publication Data

McDougall, Len.
  Tracking and reading sign : a guide to mastering the original forensic science / Len McDougall.
     p. cm.
  ISBN 978-1-61608-006-8 (pb : alk. paper)
  1. Animal tracks--Identification. 2. Tracking and trailing. 3. Animal droppings. 4. Animal behavior. 5. Wilderness survival. I. Title.
  QL768.M46 2010
  591.47'9--dc22
                              2009050543

Printed in China

Dedicated to Del Morris and the International Society
of Professional Trackers, an organization commited to
keeping alive the uniquely human ability to track, and
to using those skills associated with tracking for the
betterment and safety of humankind.

Contents

Introduction

Tracking animals—and sometimes humans—is the original forensic science, and the attraction it holds for people from every walk of life can be seen all around us, from board games such as Clue to the mystery novels of Agatha Christie and the widespread success of TV shows like *CSI*. The satisfaction we get from gathering bits of information and assembling them into a picture of what happened is instinctive. Having been denied the sharp senses common to animal predators, *Homo sapiens* learned to think abstractly. Our ancestors learned to follow the animals they preyed on by observing disturbances their passing made on the environment. A paw print, a claw scratch, scat—each of these told a story, and hunters could fit those pieces into a cogent picture of what had probably happened there. A spray of dirt behind hoof prints told of a deer that suddenly bounded away; scratch marks next to scat indicated that a coyote believed this place to be his domain; a grassy depression lined with fur marked the place where a hare mother nursed her young.

Despite its supernatural aura, tracking is more science than art, with repeatable characteristics and quantifiable data. Following the same principles as any forensics detective, a tracker learns to recognize clues and then to build a story from them by knowing how they probably came to be. A novice tracker can identify footprints, but a seasoned expert may look at the same trail and know the sex of its maker, where the animal has been, where it's going, when it might return this way, and even its state of mind. The difference between beginner and master is education, and while nothing surpasses hands-on experience, this book gets its perspective by standing on the shoulders of some of the finest trackers who ever read a trail, from the legendary Olaus J. Murie to my own Ojibwa mentor, Amos Wasageshik.

I believe I speak for those great woodsmen when I say that the best reason to become a tracker in today's world is to just plain have fun. Reading sign is an engrossing way to spend an entire day, and you needn't travel far to do it. Suburban backyards, city parks, any places frequented by wild birds and animals must yield some sign of their presence. It's a hobby whose price ranges from free to inexpensive, and anyone can participate. Not everyone will be bitten by the tracking bug, but for some (like me), the fascination for transforming a bunch of marks into a true story could blossom into a lifelong obsession.

—Len McDougall

PART ONE

Principles of Tracking
and
Reading Sign

Chapter 1

Tracks and Prints

The Quadrupedal Design

Deciphering paw and hoof impressions is fundamental to tracking, and a seasoned tracker can glean considerable information from footprints. Track size indicates an animal's approximate age, and depth yields an estimate of weight. Aside from the fact that female mammals are typically smaller than males, gender cannot be determined from tracks but might be evident through other behaviors. Front and hind tracks are usually easy to differentiate, because forefeet are larger in most species, particularly fast runners: A barrel chest permits maximum lung expansion but makes a body front heavy. Forefeet, which hit the ground together when running, require greater surface area for traction and to increase weight distribution on soft surfaces.

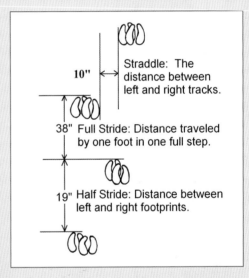

Musk ox track pattern.

Paw Anatomy

All pawed animals have segmented feet, with a heel pad and four or five toes. This arrangement has proved to be the evolutionary ideal for pawed species that make a living running, climbing, and digging. Toes can be spread wide to increase surface area on soft ground or to dig downward to maximize traction.

The number of toes in a track is a valuable identifier. Carnivores designed for fast pursuit travel on four toes. Omnivores that move with a shuffling

These wolf tracks in the mud of an evaporating beaver pond are near perfect and show the differences between broader, longer front tracks and the smaller hind paws that normally print on top of them at a casual walk.

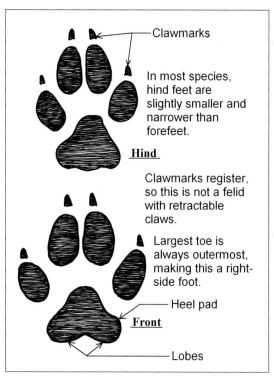

Clawmarks

In most species, hind feet are slightly smaller and narrower than forefeet.

Hind

Clawmarks register, so this is not a felid with retractable claws.

Largest toe is always outermost, making this a right-side foot.

Heel pad

Front

Lobes

Gray wolf tracks.

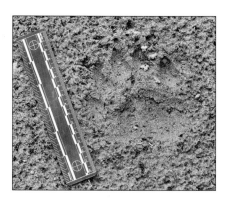

The right hind footprint of a black bear in rain-soaked sand: Forward-pointing elongated toes indicate a hind foot; the largest, most heavily imprinted outer toe is on the right, which identifies this as a right-side track; the fact that only the ball of the foot, directly behind the toes, made contact with earth says that the bear was not tired; a clean imprint, with no sand pushed to sides or rear tell of an easy, relaxed walk. Length of print, depth of impression, and the fact that this bear is unaccompanied by cubs in early summer means that this is an adult male (bear), with a 7-inch hind track—counting the heel that did not print—about five years of age, and weighing between 250–300 pounds.

gait, like bears and raccoons, have five toes on all four feet. Squirrels have four toes on the forefeet and five on the hind feet. No normal pawed mammal has fewer than four toes or more than five.

Hoof Anatomy

Hooved animals (ungulates) typically have two toes that can be splayed to form a brake on slippery ground—the horse family, with its single toe, being a notable exception. Hooved animals fall into the orders Artiodactyla (an even number of toes) and Perissodactyla (an odd number of toes). Deer, bovids, antelope, goats, and swine are cloven-hoofed, with two forward-pointing toes, most with paired dewclaws at the rear of the ankles. Most ungulates are swift runners with herbivorous diets (swine are omnivorous), and most species live in social groups.

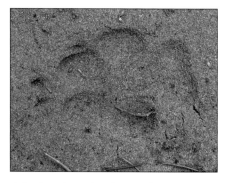

The right hind track of a walking wolf. Can you pick out the toes, heel pad, and claw marks?

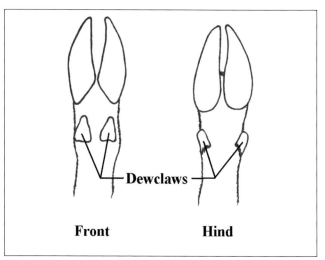

Dewclaws

Front

Hind

Whitetail deer hooves.

This pair of moose tracks, right front and right hind, might be overlooked, except for other tracks and sign along the animal's trail.

Trackers seldom have the luxury of following a clear line of tracks; most of the time tracks will be something like this deer track, which is identifiable by the size and shape of the impression left in these displaced red-pine needles.

Weight Displacement

Quadrupeds walk with weight concentrated on the outer soles, which maximizes the distance between contact points (straddle) and provides greater stability. This configuration, which is the opposite of the human design, means the outermost toe or hoof is larger and prints more heavily than the smallest innermost toe. This enables a tracker to distinguish between left and right prints.

Digitigrade

To be alert is to "be on your toes." Animals designed for quickness walk "digitigrade" fashion, body weight forward, to minimize the time required to go from motionless to top speed. This results in tracks that register most deeply at the toes, and trackers should remember that on firmer ground, only the toes may imprint. Deer, canids, and cats walk in this style.

Plantigrade

Lack of alertness can catch you "flat-footed." Plantigrade species walk flat-footed, usually have an elongated hind foot, and are not built for running speed. Most are omnivorous opportunists, with a defensive capability that deters predators: skunks have a chemical repellent, bears have brute power, porcupines have quills, and *Homo sapiens* mastered fire and weapons.

Right after a rain is an excellent time to find tracks on wet dirt roads and trails; these fisher tracks—right rear on the right, right front on the left—are welcome additions to any tracker's journal.

Chapter 2

Gaits

Track Patterns

The way all four footprints are arranged is called a "track pattern." Differences in the track patterns of walking, trotting, and running animals reveal if an animal was relaxed, had a purpose, was in flight, or was injured. Track patterns for different gaits are largely universal among quadruped mammals, with track placement for different species being similar in every gait.

How Quadrupeds Walk

Being able to see their forefeet enables animals to avoid stepping into hazards. Necessity and experience teach them to place the hind feet in the same safe location vacated by the forefoot on that side. At a walk, the forefoot and hind foot on opposite sides are brought forward at about the same time, planted securely, and used as pivot points while the opposite front and hind legs swing ahead for the next step. Pace lengths, or "stride," can vary by several inches on uneven terrain.

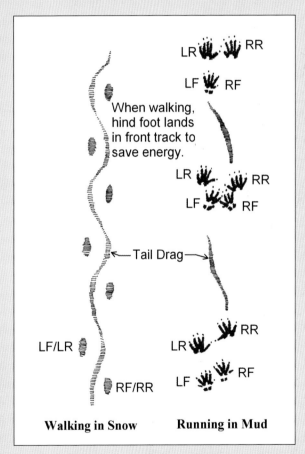

These muskrat track patterns show how foot placement changes with different gaits.

"Straddle," the distance between left and right tracks, is used to estimate an animal's width, but take note that long-legged species, especially, establish trails that are much narrower than their makers. By keeping their paws or hooves close together on narrow trails, they minimize the chance of injury on rough terrain. This enables quadrupeds to quickly create trails that permit fast, quiet travel, with

Note the foot placement of this black bear traveling at a fast walk.

minimal scent and sign, so that an 800-pound elk can travel almost silently on the trails used by smaller white-tailed or mule deer.

At a casual walk on flat ground, hind feet tend to register on top of fore prints, leaving both tracks in the same impression. Trackers should be careful not to mistake these double prints as a single footprint; hind prints will usually be discernible because they overlay fore prints.

How Quadrupeds Trot

At a trot, both hind feet and one forefoot typically print together in a roughly triangular configuration, with the remaining forefoot printing separately from the others. This ensures that three feet hit the ground simultaneously with the stability of a tripod, while the remaining forefoot acts as a fulcrum when the others are brought forward. Which forefoot prints alone indicates whether the animal is right- or left-side dominant, which may help to identify individuals.

How Quadrupeds Run

At a full-out run, quadrupeds adopt a "rocking-horse" track pattern in which forefeet are planted closely together while the rear feet are brought forward to land on either side. When the wide-apart hind feet make contact, the animal lunges forward, forefeet stretched ahead to catch it after a leap that may exceed four times its body length. One exception is the mule deer's "rubber-ball" gait, in which all four feet are kept close together under the body, where they act as springs to propel the animal in controlled bounces that can exceed ten feet.

This pronghorn antelope is exhibiting the same walking pattern seen in whitetails, elk, and other long-legged, fast-running ungulates.

Terrain Variations

Track impressions can look much different on different types of terrain, even from the same animal, at the same time, and on the same trail.

Mud

Wet mud molds itself to the contours of an object pressed into it, leaving a three-dimensional imprint that helps to determine the size of the animal and its approximate weight, details of a scar or a limp, and the definition to discern front and rear tracks.

Snow

Snow is a preferred tracking medium, as it covers everything and usually holds a clear track. But there are different types of snow, and tracks can register differently in them. One tip to remember is that the longer an animal stands motionless, the deeper and sharper the track.

Fresh, wet snow often registers a near-perfect print, but be aware that tracks in

This flying red wolf demonstrates the "rocking horse" run common to quadrupeds, where forefeet are planted close together to act as a pivot point while hind feet are brought forward and ahead of them. When hind feet make contact with the earth, the animal launches forward on powerful hind quarters, reaching out with forelegs, and the process repeats. (Photo courtesy USFWS.)

snow can "grow." Melting influences such as rain, sun, and warm air can cause a track to expand outward to half again its actual size.

Powder snow in temperatures below 20°F is dustlike and impressions may be as formless as tracks in dry sand. Stride and straddle measurements can help to identify species and size, but finding clear tracks may require following a trail to terrain where prints register more clearly.

Late-winter hardpack snow that has compressed under its own weight may also fail to show a readable track, especially when frigid temperatures give it the hardness of concrete. On frozen hardpack it may be necessary to inspect prints closely for claw marks, hoof edges, and other disturbances that can be assembled into a complete picture.

Tracks in deep snow are a series of holes, with prints hidden at the bottom. Stride lengths vary in deep powder, and gait usually consists of a series of leaps, because it is easier to jump forward than to wade through such resistance. "Depth of trough," the impression made by an animal's body, is sometimes used to guess at its size, but the best strategy is to follow a trail to terrain where footprints show clearly, because no animal prefers to struggle through deep snow.

These two running whitetails demonstrate both stages of the fast "rocking horse" running gait used by all long-legged quadrupeds. (Photo courtesy USFWS.)

Sand

Sand can register a perfect track or an unidentifiable impression. In dry beach sand, an animal's tracks may be little more than small craters, while wet sand can yield a perfect track. Measuring stride and straddle between craters helps to identify their maker.

When footprints are obscure, trackers should follow a trail to soil that holds a track's details. Damp shorelines are good places to find prints that may be defined well enough to show scarred toes, chipped hooves, or broken claws that can identify not only species but individuals.

Forest Humus

As Border Patrol officers learned when their strength was increased along the U.S.–Canadian border after 9/11, forests can be a tough place to track. Humus seldom registers more than a portion of any track, and what impressions are there will soon disappear. That also ensures that those tracks will be recent.

Hooved animals leave the most obvious prints, but even these may be just indentations in dead leaves. The sharper a hoof print's features, the fresher it is. Vegetation crushed underfoot helps to age a track: Wet, green plant tissue says the track is a few hours old; browning leaves and yellowed grass stems age it at more than a day; brown, dead plants will have been walked on numerous times, probably leaving a visible trail.

Pawed animals typically leave only faint impressions in humus, but often their claws will visibly displace leaves and debris. A twig or stone displaced from where it has laid long enough to make a depression indicates that it was kicked or rolled underfoot. Dry leaves that have slid away to reveal moist or differently colored leaves tell of an animal walking in the direction opposite the slide, and perforations made by nonretractable claws can be seen as evenly arrayed punctures in leaf humus.

Swamps can be easier to track in than hardwood forests, even in overgrown terrain, because moist ground is so impressionable. Sphagnum moss can hold an identifiable print for about a day, and soft, wet soil will keep clear tracks until they are erased by more tracks or washed away.

Chapter 3

Scat

Scat is composed of whatever wasn't absorbed by an animal's digestive tract, and undigested matter can tell trackers a lot about its depositor. Cougar and wolf scats, for example, are nearly identical in shape and size, encased in a spiral sheath of fur that scours intestines while protecting them from sharp objects. Breaking either apart usually reveals small bones, because both species swallow mouse-size prey whole, but if the interior of the scat contains chunks of a deer's leg bone, the predator had powerful jaws built for crushing, which rules out a cougar.

Scat Location

Scats may appear to be haphazard, but there's a purpose to every deposit. With so much of every species' communications dependent on scent, scat placement plays a vital role in marking or laying claim to a place.

This cougar scat is two months old and all soft organic matter in it has decomposed to powder, leaving behind the sheathing of deer hair that protected the animal's innards from sharp bone shards and helped to clean its colon.

Predator scats are left strategically at trail intersections as boundary markers to discourage competitors. Trackers who find predator scat on an established trail can expect to find an intersecting trail that crosses there. Boundary scats most often belong to males; females are naturally less ostentatious and tend to be less territorial unless rearing young. Scat posts serve to warn potential competitors that a territory is claimed, both visually and with an olfactory biography of the maker's gender, age, and size.

This olfactory calling card also helps to make mating males stand out during their rut. Bull elk employ scat as part of the bath of mud, urine, and scat that every contending male covers himself with to maximize his chances of being noticed. For whitetails and hares—whose scats are left at random along a spiderweb of trails that become more numerous closer to feeding areas—the advantage is that everything smells like them. If a pursuing predator loses sight of its prey for even a second, it will probably not be able to reacquire it by scent in that maze of smells.

Interpreting Diet from Scat

Some of everything that goes into a creature comes out in a usually identifiable form. Soft, black raccoon scat with a sprinkling of small whitish seeds says that the animal has been feeding in a berry patch nearby. In blueberry country (July through September), expect that scats from even carnivores will be distinctly purple, often with undigested berries throughout. Cow-pie-like moose and elk scats indicate that the animals have been eating their fill of rich vegetation (especially apples), which upsets their digestive tracts and narrows the places a tracker would look to find those animals during feeding hours. Porcupine scat pellets strung together like beads reveal that this nocturnal feeder has been grazing in green, grassy places. Cat or canine scats wrapped in a spiral of fine fur, with very small bones inside, tell of a diet of rodents, while coarse fur with large fragments of crushed leg bone inside say that this large carnivore was probably a bear or a wolf that fed on deer.

Some meat-eaters are classed as "strict" carnivores, but as this purple blueberry-filled coyote scat demonstrates, meat-eaters need some vegetation in their diets to provide nutrients and sugars not found in flesh.

A hallmark of every skilled tracker is an intimate knowledge of the animals he tracks—this muskrat scat is identifiable because muskrats are aquatic, they eat mostly aquatic plants, and they routinely deposit pellets of scat atop logs as territorial claims.

This scat is about one month old and shows how organic materials in excrement of all kinds will decay, turn white, and finally crumble to powder.

Breaking apart a scat to examine its contents more closely is a part of the tracking experience, but you should never handle a scat without gloves, because they may contain parasites harmful to humans.

Interpreting Health from Scat

Scats are an indicator of health. A bear whose scat is dry and fibrous in autumn, maybe with a mucous coating, is ill, probably not fat enough to survive the coming winter, and likely an old, arthritic individual that could be dangerous. Predator scats, especially, may contain whitish parasitic worms, or segments of larger worms, which tell that this individual's health is compromised.

While loose, watery scats don't necessarily indicate illness greater than an upset stomach, healthy scats are always formed and firm. Shape is roughly cylindrical, reflecting the shape and diameter of the sphincter muscles that produce it. An abundance of grasses, nature's own dietary fiber, in carnivore scats reveals a need to scrub undigested material from the animal's lower digestive tract and is especially prevalent with older individuals.

Never handle scat with bare hands. Infectious organisms are common in feces, including tapeworms and other organisms dangerous to humans. When breaking apart a sample to examine its contents, wear disposable plastic or nitrile gloves, and use a stick to open the deposit.

Aging Scat

Food color largely determines scat color. Purple scats are common in blueberry country, but fresh carnivore scat that is black and smells like rotted meat denotes a meal of pure meat from large prey. Crushed bones show as chunks of white or sometimes as a whitish area of coarsely powdered bone. Spherical rabbit pellets that are green tell that their maker was frightened off before it could reingest them for final digestion (a process known as cecal fermentation); completely digested scat pellets are dark brown.

Whatever color a scat is, it will lighten in color with exposure to air. Fast-decaying organics, like meat and skin, are the first to decompose, becoming paler as time passes, until those materials turn ash white and crumble. Tougher hairs, grass, and plant fibers remain intact for up to several months but also pale with age. How quickly a scat fades depends on environmental influences: in hot weather, the process can take a mere two days; colder weather can slow decay for up to several weeks; and scats left atop snow may remain fresh looking until spring thaw.

Chapter 4

Sign

Reading Sign

Reading footprints is the most romanticized part of tracking, but visible clues to following a creature's route are not limited to paw or hoof impressions. Furbearers shed and grow seasonal coats in response to seasonal temperature changes, and, especially in spring, shed fur is often caught in tree bark. Small patches of moist leaves that contrast with a dry, lighter-colored top layer must have been made by an animal; a closer look could reveal a regular series of disturbances, which can then be measured for stride and straddle and used to determine what, and even which, animal passed there. When trailing an animal afield, recognizing the visible impact it leaves on the environment can be invaluable.

Territorial Sign

Animals mark their territories to warn off competitors who might try to infringe on their resources. Scat deposits are the most common claim of ownership, but numerous other signs are employed as well.

Among carnivores, one sign of choice is claw marks. Dominant canids, from wolves to dogs, tend to scratch the earth with all four feet after relieving themselves, leaving a visual representation of how large they are and a scent signature from interdigital glands located between the toes. A bear stands erect and scratches as high up as it can reach on a tall tree, leaving large, obvious, parallel gouges that tell other bears how large and formidable it is. Cats scratch the earth after defecating in a perfunctory effort to cover the odors from their scat but leave a territorial scent from interdigital glands as they

The paired incisor scrapes in this birch tree say that there are beavers nearby; but more than that, the uppermost cut end tells us that there was three feet of snow on the ground when this tree was first cut down, while the lower cut below it was done after the snow had melted.

This red squirrel feeding station has been used many times by generations of squirrels who considered it a territorial marker—it's a matter of hours before its current owner returns.

scratch with claws extended and toes wide apart. Felids are also well known for their scratching posts on trees, especially pines with sticky, strongly scented sap that helps to hide a cat's own odors from prey.

Animals not equipped with stout claws resort to different kinds of territorial markings, like the mud-and-stick scent mounds used by beavers and muskrats to claim a section of river. Bucks and bulls of the deer family scrape their antlers against trees to advertise their size and disposition. Elk stags roll in bathtub-size mud wallows that are scented with urine and feces. Even the feisty little red squirrel marks its territory with bits of pinecone, discarded after the seed has been eaten, that eventually form a considerable pile as the squirrel feeds in that same place day after day.

Smells that can benefit a tracker in the field include urine. A human nose can detect the musky urine odor of a rutting buck's scrape or the pungent aroma of a wild cat's scent post from several yards downwind. On snow, the yellow markings left by a coyote cocking its leg against a tree or the yellow spray of a cat that backed up to the trunk to do the same are apparent from yards away.

Some sign is inadvertent. Flakes of keratin shed from a growing turtle's carapace or the feathers dropped by roosting turkeys aren't left intentionally, yet they are proof positive of those animals' presence. The furrow left by a deer as it moved through tall grasses is easy to follow, even without tracks. The sliding troughs made by otters in muddy or snow-covered riverbanks are a definite clue to their presence, and a dragged tail can by itself identify some species.

Feeding Sign

The dismembered carcass of a grown deer is a sure sign that large predators are nearby and possibly close enough to

These yellow swallowtail butterflies are among several species that are attracted to the minerals in wet animal urine, and they serve to help trackers identify territorial scent posts.

This Canada goose was taken by a wolf while nesting at night on a river's shoreline, a fact that was revealed by tracks, scats, and teeth-marks on broken bones (crushed to get the marrow inside).

resent the appearance of another meat eater. Never approach within 100 yards of the carcass of any large animal unless it has been stripped clean (use binoculars), and even then do so with utmost caution.

None of the deer or bovine families have upper front teeth, only lower incisors with a hard upper palate that makes them tear away the vegetation they eat. Unlike rodents and rabbits, whose sharp upper and lower incisors snip off plants like scissors, grazing animals leave grasses and plants with fibrous, ragged ends that are wet when fresh, becoming progressively drier and yellow, then brown or black.

Carnivores all have some vegetation in their diets, to provide nutrients not obtained from flesh, and most ingest rough grasses on occasion to help clean the digestive tract or induce vomiting. A yearly phenomenon in blueberry country is the way nearly every species' scat— even birds—turns purple from midsummer to fall. While carnivores possess sharp upper and lower incisors that should be capable of neatly clipping roughage, they also tend to tear away grasses rather than bite them off.

Think also of a species' physiology. Bears possess an efficient but convoluted intestinal tract that enables them to digest coarse foods but can be injured by sharp objects; one bear sign is a squirrel carcass that has been consumed except for the sharp-clawed feet. With less-articulate paws and a straighter digestive tract, wolves, coyotes, and foxes swallow small animals whole, ingesting food in as large a portion as can be swallowed. With wolves, large carcasses are often skinned by an anchor wolf whose canines pierce and hold through the nasal bones (rostrum) of a victim, while another wolf yanks the hide free of the meat.

Whether killed by predator or car, carcasses are normally stripped to the bone by scavengers, and the sign left on a carcass can tell a lot about what fed there. Coyotes scrape meat from bone and gnaw rib ends but lack the bite strength to crush larger bones for their marrow, the way a wolf or bear can. With cats, the bones may be wet and fresh yet stripped clean of meat by a rasplike tongue.

Predators don't like to eat large kills in the same places where they were brought down or found, and they prefer to drag or carry them into a secluded thicket. Coyotes can carry nothing larger than a turkey, but gray wolves can lock onto the spine of a 75-pound whitetail carcass and carry it a quarter mile before feeding.

Some feeding sign makes obvious changes to the environment; wild cherries are an autumn food for bears, and trees bearing them will be broken, even split apart, by the powerful animals to bring fruits within reach. Broken twigs still on the tree were probably caused by a raccoon as it reached for fruits. Clipped twig ends on the ground were nipped off by rodents (squirrels, porcupines), which then climbed down to retrieve the berries or cones.

Mating Sign

Mating sign tends to be obvious, because the goal is to attract attention from the opposite sex. From the brightly colored head of a rutting tom turkey to the urine-scented scratching posts of a lynx to the pungent odor of a wallowing bull elk, males are ostentatious. With few exceptions—like wolves and geese—males are polygamous, breeding with as many females as possible before seasonal hormones subside. Females typically maintain a low profile during mating season and feed heavily to prepare for pregnancy. Almost universally, males pursue females, sometimes to exhaustion. Fatigued males often drag their toes while walking, kicking, and scraping low obstacles that would normally be cleared. Tired male deer may also leave kicked-up divots in grass or moss.

Dens, like this recently abandoned red fox burrow, are a sure sign that the owner was, and probably still is, about; tracks in loose soil around the entrance identify its species.

Mating sign is also territorial, because territoriality and ritual combat help to ensure that only the fittest animals reproduce. Whitetail bucks create scrapes—patches of pawed-up earth scented with hormone-laden urine. Boar black bears mark territory by reaching as high as they can to claw standing trees, leaving interdigital scent from their paws and visual clues about their size and strength.

Bedding Sign

Every animal sleeps, and different species prefer different environments. By knowing a species' habits, a tracker can stalk into places where animals feel relaxed and are likely to move about. These safe places are usually overgrown, with only a few well-traveled trails that are used by every local inhabitant.

Most mammals prefer to sleep in places that are concealed but afford a good view of the surrounding terrain. For squirrels, that will be a den or arboreal nest; bears and deer lay up in dense thickets, where superb olfactory senses and noisy forest debris help to ensure that no enemy approaches undetected.

An oblong depression crushed down in tall grasses indicates that an animal slept there; it also reveals the animal's size, a rough estimate of its weight, and maybe even if it was a pregnant female. A deer-size bed of flattened leaves on a wooded hillside may have belonged to a wolf lying in ambush, and a wolf hunting large prey was probably not alone. If the bed belonged to a deer family, remember that males advertise themselves, especially during the rut, and bucks typically urinate onto the bed; nonbreeding or pregnant females avoid scenting themselves and do not normally urinate on their own beds.

Environmental Disturbances

Animals get itches; the warm spring sun causes winter fur to scratch against the skin, prompting wearers to rub it free on rough-barked trees, rocks, and even utility poles. Discarded fur can help to identify the species, and hairs caught in slivered wood or tree bark can give an estimate of height. Shed fur remains intact for several months, and the animal that lost it will likely be back that way again. Expect good tracks at scratching posts, left when the animal shoved hard against the earth while moving its body.

Buck or bull rubs, made when antlered animals shred the bark of small trees while scraping off the dead velvetlike tissue that nurtures antlers through summer, are a visible sign that male deer are around. All antlered species clean their racks to polished bone before autumn's mating season, simultaneously scenting the saplings they scrape with hormonal scents from glands located on the forehead. Desiccated brown skin with a velvety texture on one side marks rubbing sites. Rubs provide an estimate of the maker's size by how far scrape marks reach up a trunk, and there are always heavy tracks. Some branches show signs of abuse from being sparred with by antlers. Contending males may rub the same sapling, or another sapling close by, a challenge that helps to keep both males preoccupied with one another.

Chapter 5

Scents

The Role of Scents

The few smell receptors in a human's short nasal passages prohibit our species from sampling the way scents, or spoor, play a crucial part in almost every species' daily lives. But we do know from centuries of observations that animals employ and respond to odors the same way a hungry man might be drawn to the odor of food, or the way a young lady might wear perfume to enhance her attractiveness to men, or even the way people try to accomplish the same purpose by lighting matches before leaving a restroom. The big difference between scents in the animal world and our own is that animals have the olfactory tools to detect odors that our own noses cannot smell, so spoor is a big part of the way animals communicate with one another.

Territorial Scents

Territorial scents, usually urine-borne hormones or glandular secretions from the anal region, are often undetectable by the human nose. Unlike sexual scents whose purpose is to attract prospective mates, territorial scents serve as a fence that warns away trespassers.

Cat odors are easy to detect, but a male coyote that cocked its leg against a

This black bear is smelling around the cherry tree he intends to eat from to identify trespassers by their olfactory fingerprints.

tree may require a tracker to take a close-up sniff of the tree. Smelling for urine on a whitetail bed can reveal the animal's sex because bucks tend to urinate directly onto the bed; does do not. Whitetail buck urine contains information about size, sex, and more. Male canids urinate as high up on a tree as they can to maximize the appearance of tallness to potential rivals.

Mating Scents

Sex odors are intentionally strong because nature intends them to broadcast the availability of their maker over as wide an area as possible. Nearly all sexual scents have a strong musky smell that has been described as skunklike. Mating scent posts are often fragrant enough to be located by scent alone.

Danger Scents

The smell of fear is real in the animal world. Interdigital glands located between a deer's cloven hooves exude a hormonal odor that other deer recognize as fright, giving others

Most animals possess what is known as a "Jacob's Organ" at the back of their throats, a super-sensitive odor detector that actually enables them to taste the air.

Wild animals experience dimensions of sight, sound, and smell that are beyond our ability to detect, but trackers need to understand what and how wild species perceive the world around them.

warning to avoid that area. A similar interdigital excretion comes from the sweaty palms of humans who are afraid.

Camouflage Scents

Most dog owners have seen a pet rolling on something foul. This behavior, common to carnivorous mammals, is meant to fool prey into believing that a hunter moving in for the kill is already dead and therefore not a threat.

Chapter 6

Animal Behaviors

Thinking like prey is key to any tracker's success, and the importance of knowing the details of that species' behavior cannot be overstressed. Fortunately, many basics of life are generic, and these should be the first facts that a tracker commits to memory. Every animal needs water to live, so it must be part of every habitat. Plant life is crucial, both to herbivores and to the carnivores that hunt them. Adults claim an exclusive territory that contains food, water, and space for mating and rearing young, and they defend those resources against usurpers.

Life in the wild is hard, and animals living there do things the easy way, conserving energy for when it is most needed. Left unmolested, they fall into routines that make daily activities as undemanding as possible. Established trails are traveled by many species, and if an animal walked a worn path in one direction this morning, it will probably return from that direction this evening. Established trails permit quiet, leisurely travel because debris that would make noise underfoot has already been snapped, crushed, or kicked aside, and they allow fast runners to flee or pursue through tangled jungle.

Territorial Behaviors

With rare exceptions (such as armadillos), wild animals must be territorial because laying exclusive claim to an area serves vital functions in the animal world: first is possession of food and water sufficient for survival; second is a secure space in which to mate and rear progeny. Territorial instinct also prevents inbreeding that would weaken the gene pool and helps guarantee that only the most capable adults procreate.

Territories must be signed, especially at the borders, and markings must be obvious. Because the most far-reaching sense for most species is smell, markings are usually odoriferous and often visible. Having both of those characteristics, scats are the most frequently used markers. Scats are nearly always deposited at trail intersections, and a tracker who encounters scat on a hiking path should expect to find an animal trail that crosses it.

Territories are claimed by adult males and sometimes by females with young. The deer family is one exception in which the dominant animal will always be a female. Competitors for a territory's resources are met with a threat of violence; female deer resolve challenges with front-hoof kicking matches that can be brutal. Males challenge intruders, but arguments

Hierarchy is vital in the animal kingdom, and animals are constantly testing one another with body language—even occasional sparring matches—but combatants are rarely injured because that isn't conducive to survival of a species.

are usually settled through posturing and body language, because genuine fighting could seriously injure both animals.

Feeding Behaviors

Food is one commodity that all species are possessive of all the time. With the exception of parents, mates, and packs, animals do not share food. Creatures that might encroach on a food supply are regarded as enemies, and only weaker animals surrender food without a scuffle. Several species might feed from the same meadow or off the same carcass, but this is always done in a hierarchy: A wolf pack takes a deer and eats its fill, then a coyote strips off any remaining meat, and birds clean the skeleton, while squirrels and porcupines gnaw the bones for nutrients.

Carcasses with flesh still on them should never be approached (use binoculars), and the fresher the kill, the greater a tracker's caution should be. Wolf packs have surrendered kills to starving humans, but large cats are notoriously possessive of prey, and bears are likely to become aggressive in defense of a carcass. When a carcass is partially covered with scraped-up forest debris, it's a sure sign that the owner is close by and means to return.

After eating all they can from a carcass, carnivores oftentimes claim the stripped remains by depositing a scat directly onto them, probably as a territorial claim and an advertisement of hunting prowess. Wolverines scent unfinished remains with foul, musky urine that makes the meat unpalatable to other carnivores. Cats spray partially eaten carcasses for the same reason.

Mating Behaviors

Most wild species have mating seasons, or "ruts," that occur at the same time each year. Ruts are genetically timed to ensure that new generations grow up during the warmest season, when food is most plentiful. Some, like bears, mate in summer, and females carry embryos in suspended animation (stasis) until denning in early winter, when they either attach to their healthy mother's uterus or spontaneously abort if the female is underfed or sickly. A few, like the cougar, may breed in any month, but weather, availability of prey, and a mother's health still dictate when a female comes into heat.

Abnormal behaviors by mating males are typical, because they especially are driven by hormone-induced lust. Most are polygamous, impregnating as many females as possible.

The most important constant in the life of any animal is food, and even a raccoon can be violently possessive of a good meal; never approach any carcass, but observe from a distance through binoculars.

Some, like whitetail bucks, even forego eating during their annual sexual fixation. Human hunters exploit that preoccupation, because a savvy male is never more likely to make a mistake than when his mind is on sex.

Females are concerned primarily with birthing and rearing young and lose interest in sex after they sense they've become pregnant. Adult females spend most of their lives pregnant or raising offspring, and it behooves them to keep a low profile. While males employ ostentatious signals to attract mates, females usually communicate their readiness with urine-based pheromonal scent posts. Interested males must pursue females as they continue to feed heavily in preparation for pregnancy.

Bedding Behaviors

Most animals are crepuscular, being most active at dawn and dusk, when they move between feeding grounds and secluded bedding places. Most species are also nocturnal, as night is the safest time, when humans are not likely to be encountered and vehicle traffic is most visible.

Herbivores in open places generally rely on the safety of a herd, but solitary species seek out concealment for their beds. Bears, cats, hares, and coyotes are among game species with solitary lives and a preference for overgrown sleeping areas. The ideal bed is one that conceals its owner from sight and smell, where even soft-footed predators make noise when they walk, and is in a location where strong winds cannot reach. Game trails through overgrown bedding places tend to be fewer and more heavily traveled, used by numerous species, with less-obvious trails branching off to bed sites. Trails leading from feeding areas to beds are very good places to catch animals coming in to bed before dawn or leaving to feed each evening.

When stalking a bedding area, do everything slowly. Never take a step until you're certain that no animal is lying motionless in shadowed underbrush. The animal you seek is consciously hiding and instantly awakened by odors and sounds that are out of place. Spooking a trophy buck might cost you bragging rights, but happening on a sleeping bear or moose at close range can be dangerous.

Scents in Behavior

Many species communicate with sounds, but most messages in the animal world are transmitted through odors. Smell is one of the most refined senses among wild animals, and its importance ranks a close second to vision. Like radar, it serves as an early warning system for identifying hazards beyond the range of vision or hearing, before they become immediate dangers.

Urine provides an olfactory biography of its owner, carrying spoor that identifies an individual's gender, age, health, sexual readiness, and even size. A coyote knows the boundaries of a neighbor's territory because it can smell them; a rutting buck scents how many does have visited his scrape; a turkey vulture—the king of smellers—can detect carrion meals from ten miles away.

A tracker must abide by rules of smell that he or she cannot perceive. Being upwind will probably enable an animal to detect you long before you see it. Leaving bodily fluids—including sweat—near a game trail can cause it to be abandoned for several days. In cold weather, scents are weaker but dissipate slowly; in hot weather, smells spread strong and wide but fade quickly.

Body Language

An animal that encroaches on another's territory, beyond marked boundaries, either has nothing to fear (bears do not respect coyote boundaries) or means to appropriate that territory as its own. But before entering into a confrontation that could leave them both bleeding, possibly blinded, or broken, adversaries employ posturing and body language to persuade one another to withdraw peacefully.

Knowledge of body language is critical to trackers, because they, more than any other outdoorsmen, are likely to meet an animal at close range. Most large carnivores respect humans as a dangerous species and are quick to withdraw, but accurately interpreting an animal's posturing can be essential for getting out of a standoff unscathed.

Scents play an important role in the communication of nearly every species; this gray wolf is scenting himself with urine deposited onto the tree trunk.

A healthy animal that stands its ground probably has something worth protecting, such as offspring or a fresh kill. A steady stare is always a warning to back off. Some experts suggest averting your eyes to avoid looking adversarial, while many experienced woodsmen claim that appearing weak invites an attack. All experts agree that a person should never run away, because that incites every species to give chase.

Remain standing during any face-off with a wild animal; in fact, spread your jacket open or place a daypack or other object atop your head to make yourself appear larger. Different species have different body language: kneeling before a black bear is a sign of aggression, while kneeling before a gray wolf is an act of submission. Step backward the way you came, never turning your back until the animal is out of sight. Be silent so long as the animal is motionless, but shout loudly if it approaches, bearing in mind that most charges are merely a test of your resolve.

Consider body language from an animal's perspective: Tossing a hot dog to a "friendly" wolf tells the animal that you, and maybe the next camper, will surrender food when challenged. To a moose mother, we are carnivores, and no meat eater is permitted near moose calves. To a cougar, whose keen hunting instincts make it behave like a house cat, a small-framed jogger who is breathing hard is a slow-moving animal in distress.

Escape Behaviors

The goal of a fleeing animal is to get beyond visual range of whatever caused it to run away. Thick vegetation is preferred, because the most acute nose is confused by the plethora of scents within.

Surprised animals that dive into dense thickets are actually headed for an established trail, where they can race along a path that they know intimately. A tracker who knows the location of these trails can exploit that knowledge, particularly in areas of heavy human traffic.

Animals rarely expend more energy than is necessary to escape danger, and most stop as soon as they feel safe. A tracker who freezes immediately may find that the animal runs only until it can no longer see him, and then stops to look back. Having sharper vision than most creatures, a human can often see the animal when it stops, even though it cannot see the human.

Unless disturbed, all animals tend to be creatures of habit, and where a deer went into a swamp in the morning is most likely to be the same place where it emerges again that evening.

Chapter 7

Tracking Techniques

Scouting

A tracker who doesn't scout his hunting area is relying on blind luck. The objective of scouting is to establish what animals live within an area, how many live there, what they eat, where they drink, and what their normal routines are. A tracker who knows these things is consistently more successful at finding any species than one who does not.

Litmus Field

The appearance of foreign objects as small as a candy wrapper on a trail is sufficient to cause every species that travels it to choose a different route until time proves the object to be harmless. Wild animals grow old by being alert to minute changes in their environments, and a scout should always presume that every creature is on guard.

But animals cannot read tracks; they lack the cognitive abilities to recognize what is represented by impressions in the earth. They can detect and communicate through the faintest odors but marks in the ground go unnoticed. A scout can exploit this weakness by using a litmus field, or track field, so called because it reveals the passage of even mice.

Used by Border Patrol officers and bear hunters who drag bedsprings behind their trucks, a litmus field is a broken-up patch of soil made fluffy enough to register an imprint of an object that presses into its soft surface. You can make one with the tip of a stick, or, even better, a gardener's hand rake, erasing tracks already there and creating a clean slate, as it were.

Wet shoreline can be transformed into a track field, but most litmus fields will be on "runway" trails that are traveled regularly. First, scrape away any debris from a section of a trail; then, loosen the packed topsoil or snow with a rake or stick, filling in existing tracks and leaving a loose, furrowed surface that holds a clear impression. By checking the field at least once daily, noting the tracks recorded there and then erasing the field for the next passers-through, a scout-tracker can learn, sometimes within a day, what species of animals live there and their sizes and relative ages and even begin to track specific individuals.

Trail Timers

Left undisturbed, animals adopt daily routines because doing the same thing the same way at the same time every day maximizes efficiency and minimizes work. Most species are crepuscular (most active at dawn and dusk), when they move between bedding and feeding areas. A bear or moose that trods an established trail into alder thickets this morning will emerge from those same thickets to feed this evening, probably using the same trail. The more photographers or hunters can narrow their prey's timetables, the shorter the time they'll spend enduring cold, bugs, heat, and rain.

String Timers

String timers are a simple way to determine if and when animals are using a trail. These basic timers are made by stretching a length of dark-colored sewing thread across a trail, one end tied securely, the other wedged loosely in bark or a split twig; 100 of them can easily fit into a shirt pocket. By hanging the threads at different heights, checking and resetting them, and noting the times, you can quickly identify the species that use a trail and their timetables. You can even determine direction of travel by which way the string was pulled.

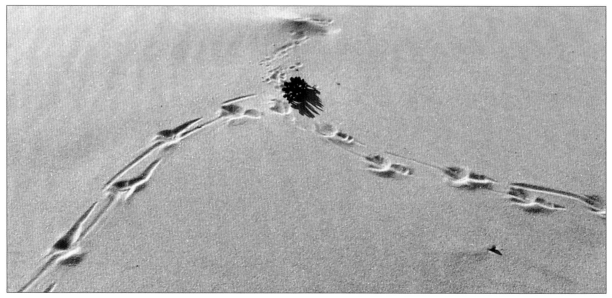

Natural tracking places, where you're most likely to find abundant tracks, include beaches and shorelines, dirt roads, and tidal flats; here a raven hopped along the beach, stopped to investigate a wind-blown pine cone, then continued on its way.

When using string timers, it pays to set many, especially at trail branches or intersections and at different heights. Take care not to scent the absorbent thread with odor-bearing chemicals—including sweat—that may be detectable by animal noses for months.

Electronic Timers

Battery-operated trail timers can record the day, date, time, and direction an animal was traveling when it passed through. From basic single-event models that trip when a string is pulled to four-plus megapixel camera models that photograph (even videotape) animals when they break a beam of light, these scouting tools range from less than $20 to more than $400.

When setting an electronic timer, take precautions against leaving scent or sign but also against hazards imposed by nature, especially cold. Conceal the unit out of the wind and within natural cover, where freezing rains or driven snow won't ice up trigger mechanisms or obscure camera lenses. Electronic components have a lower temperature threshold of –5 °F; below that, phenolic circuit boards can crack, and LCD screens can be permanently damaged.

Cold Hunting

A tracker who doesn't have the luxury of being intimate with his or her territory must employ shortcuts. The first items on your list should be a topographical map of the area, a quality map compass, and the know-how to use them as a system to analyze terrain. By knowing the typical behaviors of a species, and then balancing those against water sources, impassable obstacles, and other features on your map, you can determine where an animal lives before ever seeing the place.

"Cutting sign" is essential; if you find rabbit tracks, rabbit sign, and rabbit scat, there must be rabbits living there. Shorelines are good places to start, because animals drink at least once a day, especially in the morning, after feeding. Tracks in wet earth identify the creatures that walked there by size, weight, and, in the case of a mother with young, gender. Well-traveled deer, bear, and other game trails lead from shorelines to an animal's bedding or foraging grounds, and backtracking one of these is sure to take you closer to where an animal feels secure enough to sleep.

Tracker's Field Kit

The following list is compiled from equipment that the author carries in his tracker's outfit. This list is meant to be a guide to determining what tools you might use to outfit your own tracking field kit, but it should not be construed

Aids to scouting an area to determine the kind and numbers of resident fauna include trail cameras that are triggered by motion sensors when an animal passes.

Every animal needs water, and local shorelines can reveal a great deal about the species, habits, and population densities of animals in a particular area.

as a roster of must-have products. Each item presented here has proved to be useful in the field, not all of the time or in every season or environment, but most of the time in most situations. A winter tracker might need to carry air-activated hand warmer packets to keep water or beverages from freezing, but these would just be extra weight to a summer tracker. Add to or subtract from this list at your discretion. Items that are essential for every situation are marked by a star (★).

Part of the adventure of tracking is visiting places where few others go and and where the wildest animals are found, and that means being prepared with the tools and clothing needed to cope with wilderness.

Likewise, equipment that has been mentioned by brand or model is representative of the level of quality that should be sought after, rather than as an endorsement of individual products and models that are likely to be reengineered or discontinued even before this book is printed. Look for bargains, because a full-blown do-it-all tracking system can constitute a real investment, but bear in mind that if it doesn't work, it's no bargain. A binocular that fogs from the inside is worse than useless, so even baseline models must be waterproof.

It's a fact that packing every tool and device on this list is an expensive endeavor, but it isn't true that all of these items are needed to be an effective tracker. African bushmen do very well wearing only a loincloth, but a ruler, measuring tape, and digital camera are outstanding for making easily referenced records of multiple animals. Personally, I rely heavily on the Game Finder heat detector to notify me that an animal I'm tracking is ahead, even when neither of us can yet see one another. Like any skill, the more deeply involved you get

An effective tracking outfit can be as simple as a tape measure and a notebook for jotting down sketches and memories, or it can be a sophisticated field forensics laboratory.

into the nuances of tracking, the more tools you'll find useful, even necessary. Also, products recommended here may be found less expensively, or a less expensive model may suffice, so use your own discretion.

Whenever possible, your tracking tools should be segregated into their own readily accessible kits. A tracker must often move fast—the light is fading, a storm is approaching, a wolf pack is zeroing in on a grazing deer—and having everything right at hand, without having to search for what you need, can mean the difference between elation and frustration. A daypack with lots of pockets, colored stuff sacks (available at sporting goods stores), colored-lid Gladware dishes, and an assortment of zipping plastic bags are all helpful for segregation and protection of your tools.

Equipment Bag

* ★ Daypack: Lots of pockets, internal frame, waist belt, sternum strap, padded and adjustable shoulder straps, hydration pocket; Kelty Redwing 2650.
* ★ Stuff sacks: Nylon, drawstring with cord lock, colored for coding individual kits.

Generic Gear

* ★ Pocket-size spiral notebook with pen or pencil, in zipping plastic bag.
* ★ Belt knife: Five-inch fixed-blade, sharp; Ontario Knives SpecPlus.
* ★ Gloves: Disposable, medical, or food service type, for handling scat, carcasses, four to five pairs.
* ★ Air-activated heat packets, for water bottles, four packets (if needed); HeatMax brand.
* ★ A dozen feet of duct tape wound around a pencil.
* ★ Two-ounce bottle of waterless disinfectant hand soap; Ultracept brand.

Small, comfortable, and lightweight enough to be carried all day, this Kelty hunting pack is loaded with pockets that can be segregated into individual track-casting, photography, and other kits.

Observation

- ★ Binoculars: 10×42 roof prism, waterproof, coated lenses; Pentax 10×42 DCF.
- ★ Camera: Digital, integrated zoom lens, 12 megapixel; Kodak Z950.
- ★ LED headlamp, 3-watt; Brunton L3.
- ★ Game Finder "The Finder" heat detector.
- ★ Microscope: 25× or 50× pen type; in plastic toothbrush holder Edmund Scientific Co.

Measuring Scales

- ★ Tape measure: Ten feet, locking tape, belt clip, graduated in inches and centimeters.
- ★ Ruler: Six inches, flexible, marked in inches and centimeters.

A far cry from the miners' lamps of old, LED headlamps like this SureFire Saint can provide enough light to track and work by from dusk till dawn.

Casting Kit

- ★ Plaster: One pound, in a zipping plastic bag, carried inside mixing bowl.
- ★ Spray wax: One can, kept warm, used only if necessary (wet snow); Snowprint brand.
- ★ Plastic surveyor's marking ribbon, brightly colored for marking cast locations.
- ★ Plaster mixing bowl with snap-down cover, Tupperware type, two-cup capacity or larger.
- ★ Resealable plastic dishes, low-wall Tupperware type, at least 4×4 inches, for carrying casts.
- ★ Paper towels: Partial roll, flattened, carried in plastic bread bag, for cushioning casts in dish.

Orienteering

- ★ Primary compass: Prismatic-sighted map compass, liquid-filled; Brunton 8099.
- ★ Secondary compass: Pocket type, liquid filled, worn around neck; Brunton Tag-A-Long.
- ★ GPS: 12 channel, AA powered, lighted screen, replacement batteries; Eagle Expedition II.
- ★ Map: USGS topographical, gridded with both Universal Transverse Mercator and latitude-longitude coordinates for use with GPS and magnetic compass.

Brunton's L3 LED headlamp is as bright as the spot-lights of a generation ago.

Columbia's Bugaboot (Womens' model shown) incorporates the latest in insulation materials and breathable technology to create a lightweight winter boot with the warmth of a pac-boot and the walking comfort of a hiker.

Clothing

* ★ Winter boots: Waterproof, rated to −100°F; LaCrosse RT Hardwoods HD.
* ★ Winter hiking boots: Waterproof, internal liner; Columbia Bugaboot XTM (mens/womens).
* ★ Summer boots: Hi-ankle, lace-to-toe, waterproof; Asolo Revenge GTX.

Trackers spend a lot of time on their feet, often in rugged conditions, and their footwear needs to be as comfortable as possible in any conditions that might be encountered.

* ★ Socks, all seasons: Wool or synthetic oversock with acrylic liner sock; WigWam Mills.
* ★ Base layer, winter: Synthetic, matched to temperatures, top and bottom; Medalist X-Static.
* ★ Parka shell, all seasons: Hooded, large pockets, rainproof, breathable; Columbia.
* ★ Trousers, all seasons: Six pocket, ripstop weave, GI type, dark color or camouflage.
* ★ Summer gloves: Leather or leather-and-fabric work gloves, gauntlet length, most brands.
* ★ Winter gloves: Insulated glove shells, synthetic fleece liners.
* ★ Snowshoes, hiking: 9×30 range, aluminum frame, crampons; MSR Ascent.
* ★ Snowshoes, heavy load: 10×36, aluminum frame, crampons; Atlas 1235.
* ★ Headnet: No-see-um mesh, for bug protection, glare protection, camouflage.

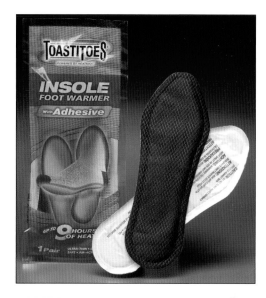

Air-activated heat packets can generate temperatures of more than 100°F for half a day, and have found many uses among modern trackers.

Chapter 8

Stalking Techniques

A tracker who is not stealthy will not be successful. Every tracker or hunter needs to move as smoothly as possible through an environment, making no unnecessary sound and leaving no scent or sign of ever having been there. A human stalker pits superior vision and intellect against his or her prey's often extremely acute senses of smell, hearing, and probably night vision. No aspect of the tracking sciences is more exhilarating than the heart-pounding satisfaction that comes from tracking, stalking, and then observing a wild creature that doesn't know you're there.

Most animals can't see colors, but they can see shapes that are out of place, so it's important to wear clothing that breaks up your outline.

What Animals See

Most mammals view their world in varying shades of blue. This isn't a weakness but a trade-off; for most animals there is little advantage in seeing bright infrareds during the day, but nocturnal species have a vital need to see at night, in the ultraviolet spectrum. Their eyes have evolved to see in darkness, with color-detecting cone cells being greatly outnumbered by light-detecting rod cells. Eagles, bees, and other species that need sharp color discrimination to hone in on food are active during daylight hours.

Stalkers need to be aware that the most nearsighted animal is acutely sensitive to

When stalking any wild animal, it's imperative that you see it before it sees you, which makes a good binocular essential to every tracker's field outfit.

This is an example of the rewards that await a skilled stalker.

motion at ranges beyond its visual clarity. A deer that cannot identify you as a human, for example, may flee because you brushed at a mosquito. Mammal eyes visually register, or "sample," their surroundings sixty times per second, and slow movements trigger less of an alarm than fast, jerky motions.

Slowing Down

The first rule of stalking is to slow down. The distinctive sound of a steady bipedal walk is alarming to all species. Squirrels and birds are notorious for announcing the presence of a human to every critter within earshot, and the alarm calls of nature's tattletales are universally understood. Wild animals rarely travel with a regular pace but pause to inspect nuances of their surroundings, stopping frequently to take in the sights, sounds, and smells before moving on. When stalking any animal, your speed should never exceed 100 yards per hour.

Even in the stark, seemingly barren landscape of a winter forest, it's difficult to pick out the outline of an upright human from the picket of vertical trees; always try to use terrain to your advantage while stalking.

There are dangers in stalking too well; always be alert and cautious to avoid startling large animals—like this feeding black bear—at close range.

Walking Indian

Foot placement is critical to stalking. A tracker must move like an animal, carefully placing each foot before gently pressing the sole against the ground. Hips and knees should be loose and slightly flexed, never tense, to absorb the shocks of walking on uneven terrain. Called "walking Indian" (by Native Americans themselves), each step forward lands softly on the outer edge of the heel, toes pointed slightly outward to maximize stance, traction, and balance. As body weight is smoothly transferred forward, the supporting foot is rolled along its outer sole to the ball of the foot and the toes, and the process is repeated with the opposite foot. This method presents your body weight to the earth over the broadest area possible, minimizing downward pressure and pressing debris gently against the earth with as few crunches and snaps as possible.

It isn't practical to stalk everywhere, but you can learn to walk Indian at faster paces. With practice you can learn to walk narrow trails almost silently at near-normal speed. Observing your own tracks can tell you where you step down too heavily, at what point your balance is weakest, and how smoothly your weight was transferred forward.

Camouflage

Human hunters have always sought to hide themselves from animals by using camouflage. Early Native Americans often wore the pelt of an animal they were hunting; this was more of a disguise than camouflage, and wearing skins actually caused hunters to accidentally shoot one another with arrows on occasion. More than five centuries after its creation by Scottish game wardens, the tattered-cloth "ghillie suit" is a standard among military snipers.

Amid the brilliant hues of a north woods in autumn, this moose stalker is difficult to see, especially for color-blind animals.

As these Odawa tribal biologists demonstrate, stalking on snowshoes is one quiet method of using terrain to an advantage.

Wind, rain, or the sound of rushing water can all be used to mask the sound of a stalker's footfalls.

Today, those are joined by computer-designed digital camouflage, Realtree, Mossy Oak, Mothwing, and other printed fabrics.

No single camouflage pattern is effective in all environments. The fundamentals of a working camouflage include loose-fitting clothing that makes a body asymmetrical and without form, wearing colors that don't contrast against surrounding terrain, and using natural foliage to complement printed camo.

Stalking under Observation

Open spaces are the toughest places to stalk. One proven hide-in-plain-sight strategy is to approach on all fours from downwind in a meandering fashion, as if you were a grazing animal. Weapons, cameras, and binoculars are likely to drag behind on the ground, so prepare them for this abuse with cases and lens covers. Use tall grass, shrubs, or whatever cover is available to hide your profile, and stop frequently, as if feeding.

The Stump Method

Grazing herbivores can be stalked using the stump method. This technique is based on the observation that feeding herbivores generally keep their heads down, vision obscured by grasses, for about five seconds before rising up to look about. By exploiting a deer's lack of visual clarity and distance perception, a stalker leaving cover can use those seconds to crawl a few feet closer before freezing. When the animal looks up again, it might scrutinize you for several minutes, but if you remain still, it will resume feeding, unable to tell that what it believes is a stump has gotten closer. With practice, this method will allow a hunter to get within twenty-five yards of grazing animals on a regular basis.

Blowing in the Wind

Many a deer hunter has lamented how an animal approached from an inconvenient direction and then stared at him, making the hunter afraid to move. A solution that has proven itself for generations is "blowing in the wind." Rather than freezing in place, the hunter begins to sway gently with the breeze (even if there is none). Gently swaying like a sapling in a breeze, not like a predator moving to strike, adds doubt in an animal's mind about the hunter being worth concern and camouflages the fact that he or she is slowly moving into shooting position with every sway.

Approaching from a fog bank is one method of using terrain and weather to good advantage.

PART TWO

Tracking
Animals in the Field

Chapter 9

Hooved Animals

Family Cervidae

The cervids, members of the deer family, are ungulates (hooved animals) of the order Artiodactyla (hooved animals with an even number of toes). All cervids have a split hoof, which is actually a pair of modified, heavily nailed toes in front and a pair of smaller toes, called dewclaws, located slightly above them at the rear of the foot. All species leave a split heart-shaped track and dewclaws may print behind the hooves in softer terrain. All species are herbivores and none have upper incisors, only a hard upper palate that causes them to tear away food plants by pinning them between incisors and the palate.

NEW WORLD MOOSE
(*Alces alces*)

The largest member of the deer family, the moose is also native to northern Europe and Russia, where it was once known as elk. It was misnamed after explorers to the New World applied that name to the first giant deer they encountered, the wapiti. The wapiti was thereafter known as the American elk, while the true American elk became the moose.

Geographic Range

Moose are found throughout the northern United States bordering Canada, throughout southern Canada and into Alaska, and downward along the Rocky Mountains into Colorado.

Habitat

Moose prefer forests with plenty of water. Pines offer protection from driving winds and snow, while willows, elkslip, and aquatic browse along shorelines provide summer browse. Biting fly and mosquito hatches of spring and early summer cause moose to migrate to higher elevations where rivers and ponds are swollen with melting snow, and strong breezes keep biting insects from landing on them.

Winter browsing includes poplar, aspen, and cottonwood bark, which scars trees with identifiable sign. Moose domains typically encompass just a few square miles, and the animals move only as needed to find a location that offers protection from weather, ample food until spring, and water. Mountain moose move to protected valleys, and forest moose go to secluded beaver ponds and floodings where spring-fed inlets never freeze entirely.

Physical Characteristics

Mass: Bulls are 1,400 pounds or more at maturity; cows are roughly 10 percent smaller than bulls.

Body: Shoulder height is 5 to 6 feet; body length is 8 to 10 feet from tip of nose to tail. Moose have long legs, a thick rump, and a broad back. Bulls carry palmated antlers from spring to early winter, when old antlers that can span 4 feet across are shed and new ones begin to grow.

The moose's face is distinctive, with a long, thick muzzle, a big nose, and a large, drooping lower lip. A fold of loose skin, or dewlap, hangs beneath the jaws of mature males, growing longer as its owner ages. Large erect ears are prominent and pointed. They have excellent senses of smell and hearing but nearsighted vision.

Tail: It is similar to the domestic cow, but shorter, about 8 inches long.

Tracks: Being heavy, moose leave clear tracks in all but the hardest soil. Split-heart hoof prints are similar to the whitetail's but more than twice the size, measuring 4 to 7 inches long, 7 to 9 inches with dewclaws, and they are unlike the more circular and concave wapiti track. On hardpacked trails only the foremost portions of hooves leave an impression, resulting in shorter tracks that can be mistaken for those of a whitetail.

Scat: Normal moose scat is typical of deer, consisting of packed brown pellets that are egg or acorn shaped, 1 to almost 2 inches long, about twice the size of whitetail or mule deer scats. Variations in shape

This three-year-old bull moose, with budding antlers still "in velvet" is feeding on grasses, horsetails, and asters in a damp ditch.

This healthy young bull carries several harmless cysts, like human warts, that are likely to freeze and fall off in the coming winter.

occur with changes in diet, with soft masses that resemble cow pies occurring when an animal is making the transition between bark and woody shrubs to succulents and fruits. A scat unique to moose is the mushroom-shaped dropping that appears most commonly in moose that have fed on long, green grasses.

Coloration: The fur is short and dark brown, becoming interspersed with gray (grizzled) as the animal ages.

Sign: Moose leave identifiable marks. The paths they plow through browsing thickets are obvious. Shrubs at trailside are broken and uprooted when bulls practice with their antlers in late summer and autumn, and there may be scraps of discarded antler velvet at these places. Moose beds and wallows are identifiable as horse-size impressions of plants and soil that have been compressed under massive weight. Moose entry and exit points into mucky bogs are marked by wide troughs.

Winter sign of moose (and elk) include gnawings in the smooth bark of poplar and other softwood trees that serve as winter foods. These trees are scabbed over with rough black bark as the wound heals.

This bull moose in full autumn antlers is preparing to take one or more mates. (Photo courtesy USFWS.)

A very protective moose mother in spring with two week-old nursing calves. (Photo courtesy of USFWS.)

Vocalizations: Moose are generally silent. A cow calling for a calf emits a soft lowing, like the mooing of a domestic cow. A mother may also issue a huffing grunt to warn off intruders. During the autumn mating season, moose become more vocal, especially amorous bulls. Rutting males are boisterous and fearless and have been known to charge people, livestock, and even automobiles. Bull moose in heat may grunt like hogs and bellow like domestic bulls. The more vulnerable cows and calves communicate more quietly.

Life span: Moose live to 10 years in the wild, up to 27 years in captivity.

The left front hoofprint of a large bull moose in a muddy grass marsh. Note how grass stems have been cut cleanly by the hoof edge under massive weight.

Diet

An adult moose requires 10 pounds of vegetation per day. Like all ruminants, moose have an efficient digestive system for processing rough vegetable fiber. Foods browsed from shorelines include pond lily, water lily, marsh marigold, horsetail, and rough grasses. Moose in Michigan's Upper Peninsula have been observed eating quantities of jewelweed (*Impatiens capensis*), a plant known best as a remedy for poison ivy. Moose swim well, and their long legs permit them to wade through deep muck, where water plants grow thickest. Wintering moose eat a rougher diet of mostly willow twigs and bark, wading through snows too deep to be negotiated by shorter deer.

The right front track of a moose with the left rear track on top of it; quadrupeds learn to place the hind foot, which they cannot see, onto the same spot the forefoot had been, thus avoiding tripping hazards.

Mating Habits

Moose are sexually mature at two years. Mating occurs from September through October, with cows remaining in heat for thirty days. Cows initiate rutting with sexual pheromones in their urine and from tarsal glands inside the knees of the hind legs. Male moose become territorial during the rut, and their behavior toward intruders can be hostile.

Cow moose undergo an eight-month gestation period before giving birth to one or two unspotted calves in April or May. Newborn calves can outrun a human at two days old and can keep up with their mother by three weeks. Weaning occurs at five months, in September or October. Moose calves stay with their mother for at least a year after birth, until the next calves are born.

These formless masses, large in comparison to the darker whitetail scat pellets around them, are the aging scats of a large bull moose whose diet has consisted of succulent aquatic plants, and a little mud.

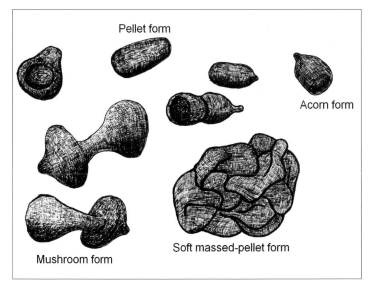

Various forms of moose scats.

Pellet form

Acorn form

Mushroom form

Soft massed-pellet form

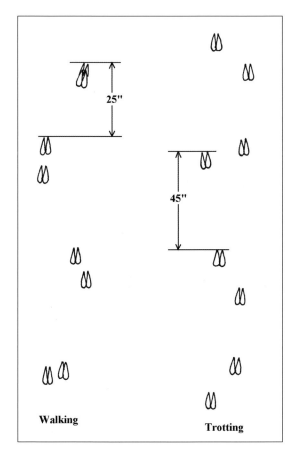

25"

45"

Walking

Trotting

6.0"

Dewclaws

Hind track overlays front track at a casual walk, a learned habit that helps keep hind feet from tripping over obstacles.

As a moose's gait changes, so does its track pattern.

Moose tracks.

Behaviorisms

Moose are most active at dawn and dusk (crepuscular) and are mostly nocturnal. Preferred bedding areas are places that have concealing vegetation and a plethora of scents to confuse predator noses. Adult moose are solitary, but two or more may feed in a particularly lush spot.

Moose are generally not migratory, but in Russia, moose are known to journey 200 miles between summer and winter habitats. Strong swimmers, they can cross swollen rivers and traverse deep snow.

Moose mothers are protective of calves, and with a running speed of 35 miles per hour, they are dangerous to all predators. Sharp front hooves are the primary weapons of either sex, although antlered bulls may also use their heads.

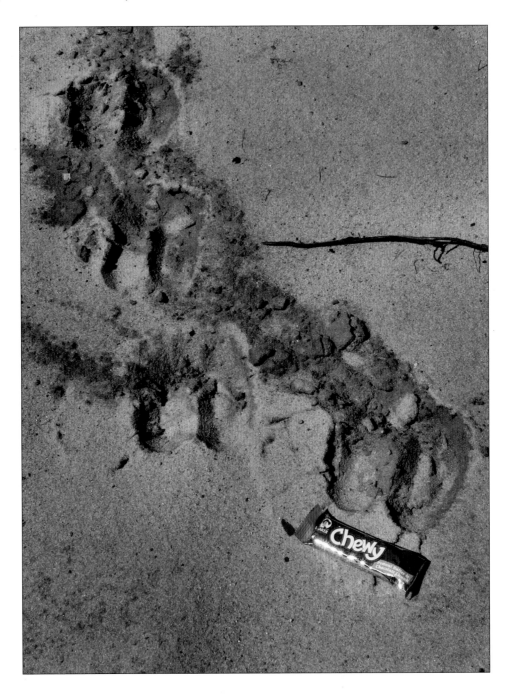

This moose stopped, looked about, and took a short, tentative step in riverbank sand that that been rained on, dried, and crusted over, with finer loose sand below.

WAPITI, OR AMERICAN ELK
(*Cervus elaphus*)

Cousin of the European red deer, the wapiti is second in size only to the moose. This large ungulate once roamed across what is now the United States, but, with little fear of predators, human or otherwise, elk made easy targets, and native populations were hunted to extinction in Indiana (1830), Ohio (1838), New York (1847), and Pennsylvania (1867). Protection came too late to save the eastern subspecies of forest-dwelling elk, *Cervus elaphus canadensis*, which is now extinct. Efforts to transplant elk to the eastern United States from the West were attempted on three occasions, with limited success.

Geographic Range

Wapiti were once common throughout the Northern Hemisphere, but today large populations are found only in western North America, from Canada down through the Rocky Mountains to New Mexico. Small populations are also found in Kentucky, Michigan, and Pennsylvania. Asia and Europe are home to a subspecies of elk known as red deer, or roebuck.

A bull elk with half-grown, velvet-covered antlers cools itself in a river on a hot July day.

Essentially a mass of soft pellets, this elk scat denotes a succulent diet of fresh green plants.

Habitat

Elk prefer open prairies where their good vision permits detection of threats by sight and scent, but the species has learned to become comfortable in forests. Elk have a greater tendency to migrate than white-tailed or mule deer.

Physical Characteristics

Mass: Elk are 900 to 1,100 pounds. Males are generally 20 percent larger than females.

Body: Shoulder height is 4.5 to 5 feet; length is 6 to 9 feet. Elk are stocky and barrel shaped, with muscular humps at the shoulders and flank. Hindquarters are higher than the shoulders, creating a jacked-up silhouette.

Tail: The tail is short and surrounded by a dark-bordered blond patch that covers most of the rump in an inverted teardrop shape.

Tracks: Tracks are 4 to 4.5 inches long, discounting dewclaws, cloven and much rounder than those of moose or deer. Hooves are concave, resulting in track impressions that are deepest around their outer perimeters.

Scat: Scat is dark brown pellets, egg or acorn shaped, 0.75 to 1 inch long.

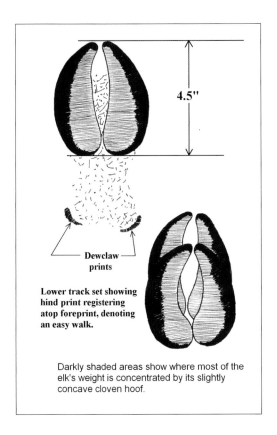

4.5"

Dewclaw prints

Lower track set showing hind print registering atop foreprint, denoting an easy walk.

Darkly shaded areas show where most of the elk's weight is concentrated by its slightly concave cloven hoof.

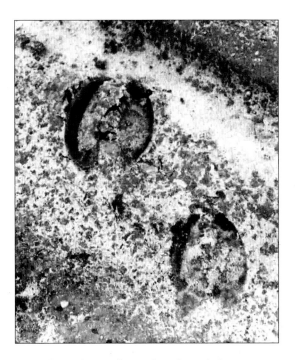

Note how these elk tracks (front left at top, hind left at bottom) are impressed most heavily around the outer edges, denoting the wapiti's concave cloven hooves, which make tracks similar to those of the caribou.

A walking elk track pattern on a damp sandy road.

Coloration: Known as the ghost of the forest, the wapiti has a dark brown head, neck, and legs, with a blond body that lends a ghostly appearance in twilight. A blond rump patch provides a visual beacon for herd members to follow.

Sign: Sign includes mud wallows, which are bathtub-size depressions created by rolling in wet earth to dislodge fur and parasites or to scent bulls with their own urine in rutting season. Wapiti feed on the smooth bark of poplar, aspen, and cottonwood trees in winter, leaving trunks scarred with bottom-teeth-only scrapes that heal as rough black-bark scabs.

Vocalizations: Best known is the bugle call of a mature rutting bull. This loud, high-pitched call, intended to be heard by receptive cows over long distances, begins as a low grunt, then abruptly becomes a hollow squeal that spans several seconds and repeats two or three times. Breeding males make coarse grunting and growling sounds, reminiscent of domestic cattle. The alarm call used by either sex is a piercing squeal. Cowlike mooing between mothers and calves keeps them close to one another.

Outside of the October-November mating season (rut), bull and cow elk live separately in same-sex herds, but in any herd a dominant cow is the alpha leader.

Life span: Elk live ten years in the wild, longer in captivity.

Diet

The elk's diet is herbivorous but varied. They eat many types of grasses and forbs, marshland plants such as marsh marigold, and the namesake elkslip. In winter the diet includes bark, twigs, and buds of aspen, poplar, beech, basswood, and evergreens. Elk are ruminants, feeding and then retiring to a resting place where the partially digested cud in their primary stomach is regurgitated to be rechewed and broken down further into usable nutrients.

Mating Habits

Both genders reach sexual maturity at sixteen months, but bulls under two years will probably not mate because of competition from stronger males. Mating season begins in late August and goes through September, with a gathering of mature bulls and cows, peaking in October and

This handsome bull in December will be shedding its polished antlers in a few days, and another set will begin growing almost immediately.

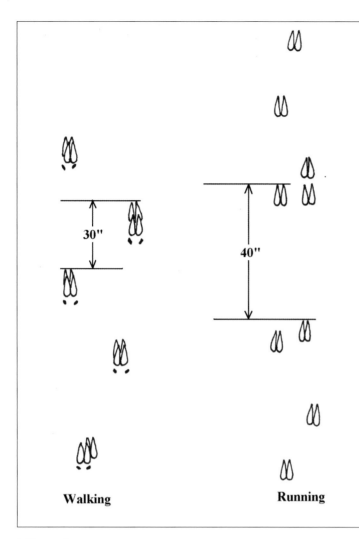

Walking   **Running**

30"   40"

Elk track patterns.

November, when actual mating occurs. Cows initiate the mating period by emitting pheromonal scents. Bull elk are known for the harems they gather, but harems are usually maternal families consisting of a dominant female and her offspring. A typical harem consists of one bull, six adult cows, and four calves.

Courtship battles between rutting bulls are shoving matches in which competitors lock antlers and attempt to shove one another's heads to the ground, whereupon the weaker animal withdraws. The objective isn't to harm an opponent, although injuries sometimes result.

Bull elk mate as many cows as possible before the rut ends. Gestation is eight to nine months, with a single 35-pound spotted calf being born in April or May. If food is abundant, cows might have twins, but this

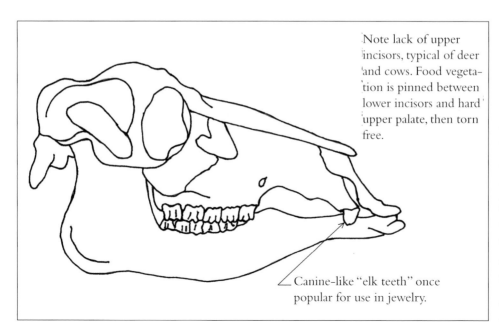

Note lack of upper incisors, typical of deer and cows. Food vegetation is pinned between lower incisors and hard upper palate, then torn free.

Canine-like "elk teeth" once popular for use in jewelry.

Note that the wapiti, like all deer, lacks upper incisors, and must tear food plants free, rather than biting them off cleanly—trackers should be alert for raggedly torn grasses and plant stems.

is abnormal. Newborn calves and mothers live separately from the herd for about two weeks, and calves are weaned at about sixty days. Male calves leave their mothers at two years, often by banishment. Females may stay with the family herd for their entire lives.

Behaviorisms

The most social of deer, wapiti spend their lives in herds. Except for mating season, adults run in same-sex herds of males and females that may number several dozen. The dominant animal in every mixed-sex herd is always a cow. Bachelor herds get along well and commonly accept strangers into their company. Cows are less accepting of strangers. Cow and bachelor herds may share the same feeding areas, but the sexes do not socialize outside of the rut. If alarmed, a mixed gathering of elk will flee in two same-sex herds.

Dominant cows are more territorial than bulls at all times of year. Territorial battles aren't common, but matriarchs protect territories against usurpers, and fights between cows are more violent than mating contests among bulls.

WHITE-TAILED DEER
(*Odocoileus virginianus*)

Known alternately as the Virginia or flagtail deer, the whitetail is a popular game animal whose financial value has spawned an entire hunting industry. No animal has been more researched, because no other game is so commercially valuable. Threatened by unrestricted hunting until the 1940s, whitetails have made a strong comeback, with some estimates ranging as high as 26 million animals in the United States alone.

Geographic Range

Common throughout the United States, whitetails inhabit all but the most arid regions, extending northward to southern Canada. Southern range includes Mexico, Central America, and northern South America.

The tracks of a doe and her fawn going to a river to drink, then returning to the forest.

Habitat

Whitetails can live in any habitat with sufficient browse, water, and concealment. They often graze in groups in open places. The species' efficient digestive system can metabolize rough vegetable fibers, even bark and twigs. The least migratory deer, a typical whitetail, spends its entire life in an area of about one square mile, moving only between open feeding and concealed bedding places. The animals are intimately familiar with every facet of their habitat.

Physical Characteristics

Mass: Whitetails are generally 150 to 200 pounds, with animals exceeding 300 pounds in the far north. Subspecies such as the Key deer of Florida and the Coues deer of Arizona average 50 pounds and 75 pounds, respectively.

Body: These deer are muscular and less barrel-shaped than other deer species, 4 to 7 feet from chest to rump. Shoulder height is 3 to 4 feet. Their powerful hindquarters and strong, slender legs propel them at speeds in excess of 30 miles per hour. Whitetail antlers have a single main tine, or beam, from which single-point tines extend. Antlers are usually shed in January and begin to grow again in April. Interdigital scent glands between hoof halves carry signature and alarm scents. At two years, bucks grow mature, tined antlers. Metatarsal glands on the outside of each hind leg and a larger tarsal gland on the inside of each hind knee are used for olfactory communication, with musk from them becoming especially pungent during mating season.

Tail: The tail is 4 to 5 inches long and brown on top with white underside. The tail is held erect when the deer is fleeing, exposing its white underside and giving rise to the common name, flagtail.

Tracks: Cloven hooves leave a split-heart impression when the toes are together, with two dewclaws behind and slightly above. Length is 3 to 3.5 inches without dewclaws.

Scat: Scat is typically oval-shaped pellets, sometimes acorn shaped, 0.5 to 0.75 inches long, and a dark brown color, lightening with age.

Coloration: The coat is reddish in summer, gray in winter. The chest and belly are white. Nose is black with a white band running around the muzzle; chin is white; and white circles are around the eyes.

This newborn fawn's mother was killed by a car just a few yards away; unable to survive on its own, the fawn was spared a lingering death by hungry coyotes with their own young to feed.

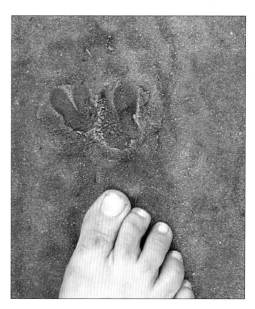

These small, rounded hoofprints are typical of newborn whitetail fawns.

This fresh whitetail scat deposit shows the variety of shapes the normal pellet form can have.

Whitetail track in soft mud showing dewclaw imprints as round holes to the rear.

Sign: Sign includes raggedly torn grasses. Saplings with bark scraped from them by a buck's antlers (rubs) are seen especially in early autumn. Patches of urine-scented pawed-up earth, called scrapes, are seen during the mating season. Lower branches of cedars and pines are stripped of foliage.

This left front whitetail track was made in wet sand during a rainstorm.

Vocalizations: Whitetails are normally silent. The alarm call is a forceful exhalation, like a sudden release of pressurized air. Does bleat softly to fawns, but the sound carries only a few yards. Mortally wounded deer bleat with goatlike sounds.

Life span: Whitetails live eight years in the wild, up to twenty years in captivity.

An adult whitetail buck with mature antlers in November. (Photo courtesy USFWS.)

Diet

Whitetails are generally nocturnal, with crepuscular feeding patterns. They tend to visit water sources in early morning, after feeding. Summer foods include grasses, alfalfa, clover, elkslip, and aquatic plants. Winter browse consists of buds and tender twigs of evergreen trees, especially cedars, as well as the bark and buds of staghorn sumac, river willow, beech, and dead grasses found in hummocks along stream- and riverbanks. In more arid country they can subsist on prickly pear, yucca, and tough, fibrous shrubs.

Mating Habits

Mating season begins in September and October with a preestrus rutting, during which bucks polish their antlers against trees and advertise sexual availability with urine-scented scrapes of pawed-up earth. During this period bucks spar with one another, usually far back in the woods, in elimination rounds that determine which is strongest. Battles are shoving matches in which contenders lock antlers and push until one withdraws. Occasional injuries result, and in rare instances both bucks have died because their antlers became inextricably locked, but the intent is never to injure an opponent, just to drive it away.

When mating begins in mid-October, bucks will have established their territories. Until the rut ends in late November (December in warmer southern regions), breeding males are

Whitetails are the most widespread and adaptable American deer.

fixated on mating and may be active anytime. Does, which may mate in their first year, play a passive role, depositing pheromone-laden urine onto a buck's scrape as they travel between feeding and bedding areas. Pregnant does need to gain body fat to survive a winter of pregnancy, so bucks check their scrapes frequently, pursuing does who leave messages.

Newborn whitetail fawns are surprisingly well camouflaged in their spotted coats.

Whitetail bucks are polygamous, mating as many does as possible during the 30- to 45-day rut. Bucks may remain with one female for several days, until she comes into estrus, but after mating, the male moves on. Does are in heat for a single day; if a doe goes unmated during her day of fertility, she comes into heat again approximately twenty-eight days later. Should this second heat pass with a doe still not becoming pregnant, she will not come into heat again until the following October.

Gestation lasts through winter, with a duration of six to seven months. Does bred for the first time normally give birth to a single spotted fawn in April or May, with twins being the norm thereafter, sometimes triplets if food is abundant. Fawns walk within hours of being

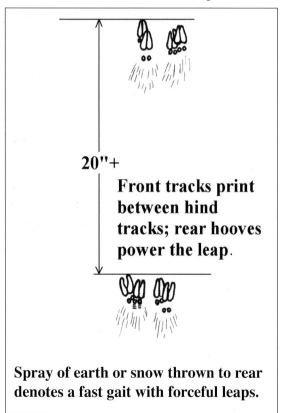

20"+

Front tracks print between hind tracks; rear hooves power the leap.

Spray of earth or snow thrown to rear denotes a fast gait with forceful leaps.

Whitetail deer leaping track pattern.

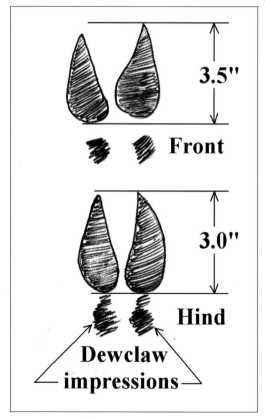

3.5"

Front

3.0"

Hind

Dewclaw impressions

Whitetail tracks.

born and within a week begin nibbling on vegetation. Mothers leave fawns hidden in grasses or underbrush while they graze nearby, checking on them frequently, and eating their feces to prevent predators from scenting them.

If a carnivore approaches a hidden fawn, the mother tries to distract it and lead it away, even feigning injury to keep the predator's interest. Weaning occurs at six weeks, but fawns remain with their mothers for the rest of the summer and sometimes through the winter, even though mothers are likely to become pregnant again.

Whitetail walking track pattern showing that hind hoof (right) sometimes registers ahead of front foot.

Behaviorisms

Whitetails are nocturnal, traveling from secluded bedding areas to feeding places at dusk, then returning to the safety of dense forest at dawn. They may move about within the seclusion of bedding areas during the day, and especially in spring, groups might graze in the open during daylight hours.

When winter snows cover ground plants, whitetails move into protected yards where pines and especially cedars provide windbreak and browse. In most places, winter yards are also summer bedding areas, enabling deer to use established trails year-round.

Whitetail does are the most dominant deer, and they are more territorial than bucks because survival demands securing a domain with food, water, and shelter. Territorial disputes between does are settled with flailing hooves and are often violent.

Whitetail deer are mostly solitary, but an abundance of food, especially crops, can cause

them to herd in large numbers. Agriculture causes whitetail populations to explode in farming regions where predatory species are unwelcome, sometimes resulting in overpopulation, disease, and an increase in car–deer accidents.

This form of whitetail scat is actually a mass of soft pellets, caused by eating rich succulents.

MULE DEER
(*Odocoileus hemionus*)

Mule deer are close cousins of the whitetail but inhabit only the western part of the United States, where migrating whitetails have begun to overlap their territories in recent years. Subspecies include the black-tailed deer of America's northwest coast.

Geographic Range

Mule deer are found from southwestern Saskatchewan through central North and South Dakota, Nebraska, Kansas, and western Texas, with sightings in Minnesota, Iowa, and Missouri. Gaps in population occur in arid regions of Nevada, California, Arizona, and the Great Salt Lake desert.

Habitat

O. hemionus occupies a range of habitats, including California chaparral, the Mojave Desert, semidesert shrub regions, the Great Plains, the Colorado Plateau shrubland and forest, the Great Basin, and the Canadian boreal forest. Mulies prefer open grassland for grazing and are seldom found in deep woods.

Physical Characteristics

Mass: Mulies range from 110 to more than 400 pounds. Males are 25 percent larger than females.

This all-doe herd of mule deer, comprised mostly of related offspring and siblings, is an example of how males and females in the Deer Family tend to remain segregated except during the autumn mating season.

Body: Mule deer are stocky, barrel shaped, and 4 to 6 feet long; shoulder height is 3 feet; ears are large and mulelike, 4 to 6 inches long. Antler spread is up to 4 feet, with the main beam forking into points, rather than individual tines growing from the main beam. Adapted to open country, *O. hemionus* has good distance vision.

Tail: The tail is 5 to 9 inches long, dark brown or black above, white below, tipped with a black or sometimes white tuft (depending on subspecies).

Tracks: Tracks are nearly identical to the split-heart print of the whitetail but usually larger in adults, measuring about 3.5 inches long, discounting dewclaws.

Scat: Scat is typically deerlike, pellet or acorn shaped, with individual pellets averaging about 0.5 to 0.75 inches long. Sometimes pellets will be massed together when browse has been succulent.

Coloration: Fur is dark brown to red during summer, becoming more gray in winter. The rump patch is white in younger individuals and yellows as the animal ages. The throat patch is white. A dark V-shaped mark that is more conspicuous in males than females extends from between the eyes upward to the top of the head.

Sign: Sign includes saplings with bark scraped by bucks rubbing their antlers. Bucks make

Mule deer track patterns. Note this species' feet-together "rubberball" bounding run, which is unique among North American deer.

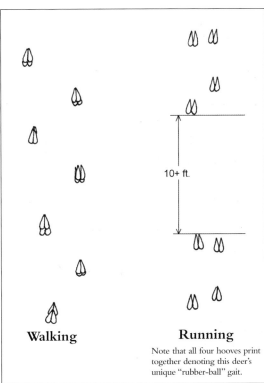

Walking

Running

10+ ft.

Note that all four hooves print together denoting this deer's unique "rubber-ball" gait.

urine-scented scrapes during the rut. Both sexes wallow in mud like elk, but depressions are smaller.

Vocalizations: Alarm is similar to the blowing of a whitetail but more prolonged, ending with a high-pitched whistle. Mule deer are vocal when grazing together, communicating softly with grunts, snorts, mooing sounds, and low squeals.

Life span: Mule deer live about ten years in the wild.

Diet

Cud-chewing ruminants like other deer, mule deer have a slightly less efficient digestive system than their cousins, requiring more easily digestible green plants in their diet. To counter a lack of green browse in winter, mule deer feed with more urgency than other deer throughout summer to put on enough fat to sustain them through winter. Green grasses, acorns, legume seeds, and berries and fleshy fruits are among the preferred foods.

Mating Habits

Mule deer breed slightly later than whitetails, beginning in October and peaking from November through December. Like whitetails, bucks create urine-scented scrapes of pawed-up earth that receptive does urinate onto as they pass between feeding and

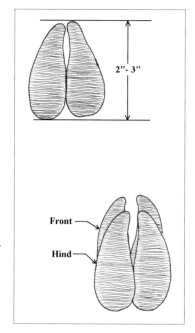

Mule deer tracks showing the split-heart cloven hoof common to all deer species, and the way hind feet are placed into front tracks during a normal casual walk.

Fresh mule deer scat shows the same pellet form exhibited by all deer species, from moose to whitetails. Ball of compressed pellets on the right indicates a rich diet of succulent greens.

bedding areas. Males are polygamous, having more than one mate per breeding season, and there is no bond between mates.

Bucks competing for mates lock antlers and shove hard against one another until the weaker opponent withdraws. Injuries sometimes occur, but the objective is to establish which is the stronger, not to harm one another.

Mule deer does are less likely to mate in their first year than whitetail does. First and second births usually produce a single fawn, with twins being the norm thereafter. Gestation lasts 29 weeks, with most fawns born mid-June to

Mule deer are the whitetail's western cousin, identifiable from a distance by their large, mule-like ears.

early July. Fawns weigh 6 to 10 pounds at birth, with twins typically weighing less than singles and males being slightly heavier than females. Fawns can walk within a few hours of birth and begin nibbling vegetation within weeks. Fawns are weaned by 16 weeks and attain full skeletal development at 3 years for females, 4 years for males; both continue to grow until the ages of 8 and 10 years, respectively.

Behaviorisms

Mule deer prefer a small home range but migrate when conditions demand. Two-year-old bucks are driven off by mothers to prevent inbreeding. Seasonal travel may be prompted by biting flies, deep snow, and drought.

Mule deer bed down during daylight in concealing thickets but are less shy about napping in the open than whitetails. Predators include cougars and wolves, with bears and coyotes preying on fawns. Mulies can see predators from as far away as 400 yards, and their bounding, feet-together, "rubber-ball" run of more than 30 miles per hour makes them hard to get hold of.

In winter, mule deer browse on commercially important trees such as the Douglas fir and Ponderosa pine. This has prompted state governments to buy tracts of land that provide suitable winter habitat.

O. hemionus is susceptible to numerous viral, bacterial, and parasitic diseases. Gastrointestinal worms are common, and infection by parasitic meningeal worms causes permanent neurological harm. Free-range livestock may infect mule deer that graze the same pastures with hoof-and-mouth disease or bovine tuberculosis.

CARIBOU
(*Rangifer tarandus*)

Best known as reindeer, caribou have been domesticated to pull sleighs and wagons, as well as for their milk, and are still an important source of food in arctic cultures.

Geographic Range

Caribou were once native to all northern latitudes, but extensive hunting drove this most northern deer from much of its original range. Large herds are still found in Alaska, Canada, Scandinavia, and Russia; unrestricted hunting is no longer allowed anywhere.

Habitat

Caribou are most at home in arctic tundra, where they migrate long distances with changing seasons and availability of food. They can adapt to temperate forests but require cold winters.

Physical Characteristics

Mass: Bulls weigh from 275 to 600 pounds; females weigh from 150 to 300 pounds.

Body: Shoulder height is 3 to 3.5 feet; length is 4.5 to 7 feet. Caribou are stocky, with thick legs and abnormally large knee joints, and have a large snout and nose pad. Both sexes are antlered, but males carry identifiably larger antlers.

Tail: The tail is 4 to 6 inches long, dark on top, white below.

Tracks: Large cloven hooves leave round impressions, 4 to 5 inches long; males make larger tracks than females. The feet are slightly broader than they are long and flat with deeply cleft hooves. The pad between hoof halves expands in summer to provide better traction

Adult bull caribou in early autumn; bloody tissue at end of brow tine is a remnant of the "velvet" that nourishes antlers during growth.

Like all cervids, caribou shed their antlers in early winter, after the rut; unlike other deer, both males and females grow antlers.

against soft terrain but shrinks in winter to conserve heat.

Scat: Scat is acorn-shaped pellets, about 0.5 inch long, sometimes clumped together in a mass when the animal has fed on succulent browse.

Coloration: The coat is heavy with dense, woolly underfur. Coat color is brown to olive, with whitish chest, buttocks, and legs. Coloration varies with geography; animals in Greenland and northeastern Canada are nearly white.

Sign: Browsed reindeer moss (*Cladina rangiferina*) lichens are a staple in the caribou diet. Shed antlers are found on open tundra.

Vocalizations: Caribou make grunts, squeals, and whistles, especially during migrations. Cows moo softly to young calves. Caribou have thick tendons that snap across a bone in the foot when they walk, producing a clicking sound (alluded to in the Christmas carol lyrics, "Up on the housetop, click, click, click").

Life span: Caribou live five years in the wild, up to thirteen years in captivity.

Diet

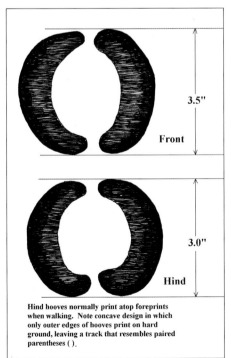

3.5"

Front

3.0"

Hind

Hind hooves normally print atop foreprints when walking. Note concave design in which only outer edges of hooves print on hard ground, leaving a track that resembles paired parentheses ( ).

Caribou are herbivores and ruminants that can digest most types of vegetation, including green leaves, evergreen buds and foliage, and small twigs. When other browse is unavailable, caribou may feed predominantly on their namesake reindeer moss, a hardy lichen that grows in carpetlike masses and is common to open, barren places around the globe.

Mating Habits

Mating season occurs throughout October, with northernmost herds rutting earliest. Both sexes can breed at two years, but competition normally prevents males from mating until age three.

Cows are seasonally polyestrous; those not impregnated during the first ten-day period of estrus will come

Caribou hoofprints as they might appear on firm ground (dewclaws do not register). Note rounded form.

Caribou migrate in sometimes vast herds in spring and in autumn.

Unique among deer, caribou hooves are extra-large and rounded to maximize weight displacement (like snowshoes) and traction on snow.

into heat again ten to fifteen days later. Caribou bulls gather harems whose size may exceed twelve cows.

In May or June, after a gestation of eight months, a single calf is born. Twins may occur if food is abundant, but they are not common. Calves weigh 12 to 19 pounds at birth; they can follow the herd within an hour and can outrun a human within a day.

Behaviorisms

Caribou are diurnal (active during daylight) and gregarious, forming herds that can number from 10 to more than 1,000 individuals—as many as 200,000 animals during seasonal migrations. Caribou are the most migratory deer, traveling up to 1,000 miles between northern summer habitats to southern winter pastures. Migrations happen abruptly, with smaller groups coalescing into vast herds that can number 20,000 animals per square mile and travel 30 miles per day.

Caribou bull in late summer, with grown antlers still covered by velvet.

Caribou scat resembles that of other deer, being pellet-formed with a normal diet, sometimes massed or soft when the diet has been rich in succulents.

Caribou are the fastest-running deer, able to sprint at 50 miles per hour for short distances, and healthy adults can quickly outdistance their greatest predator, the arctic wolf. They cannot so easily escape rifles, and by the 1600s, they had been hunted to extinction over most of their European range; by the 20th century, they had become scarce over much of their Canadian range. Presently there are thirty wild herds in North America, the smallest in Idaho and Washington, numbering about thirty animals each. The largest herds, in Canada and Alaska, number more than 50,000. Hunting laws have been enacted to protect existing populations.

Caribou track pattern, trotting.

Family Suidae

Family Suidae is composed of 16 species of hogs in 8 genera. Suids originated in southern Eurasia, on large remote islands such as those in the Philippines, and throughout Africa. Humans introduced *Sus scrofa*, the wild boar from which domesticated pigs were bred, in nonnative habitats around the globe, including North America, New Zealand, Australia, and New Guinea. Fossilized evidence of suids has been discovered from the Oligocene period (30 million years BC) in Europe and Asia and from the Miocene period (15 million years BC) in Africa.

WILD PIG
(*Sus scrofa*)

The true wild boar of Eurasia is the ancestor of all domestic swine. They share most behavioral and physical characteristics and have been transplanted as game and farm animals around the world since before the Middle Ages. Wild boars and domestic pigs interbreed freely, and where both exist, they have hybridized into a third type of swine that shares the traits of both.

Geographic Range

Wild pigs are very adaptable, and in many regions domestic hogs have escaped captivity to become part of local ecosystems, often with severe negative impact on native species. *Sus scrofa*, the wild boar from which all domestic pigs were spawned in approximately 3000 BC, occupies the largest range.

Originally there were no pigs in the Americas. Peccaries were found in South America, Mexico, and the southwestern United States but are not considered true swine. The first domestic pigs arrived with European immigrants but were unable to survive in the vast wilderness of the New World. In 1893, fifty wild boars were transplanted from Germany's Black Forest to a hunting preserve in New Hampshire's Blue Mountains. These were followed in 1910 by a release of Russian wild boars in North Carolina, another in 1925 near Monterey, California, with a few released on California's Santa Cruz Island.

Habitat

Sus scrofa is found in a variety of habitats, most typically where acorns, grasses, and roots are abundant. Short legs make swine poorly suited to deep snow, and none are sufficiently furred to endure prolonged subfreezing temperatures. Temperatures below 50°F are uncomfortably cold to wild pigs, although many survive in places where there is mild snowfall. Conversely, swine cannot tolerate hot climates, where lack of a protective coat makes them prone to sunburn and heatstroke. During hot weather, pigs seek shade during the day and wallow in mud to cool themselves.

Physical Characteristics

Mass: Wild pigs weigh from 160 to 450 pounds, occasionally weighing more than 1,000 pounds. Females are about 20 percent smaller.

Body: The body is barrel-shaped and very stout, with short, thick legs. Body length is 4.5 to 6 feet; shoulder height is up to 3 feet. The head is large with a short, massive neck and long muzzle ending in a flat disk-shaped snout with large nostrils. Eyes are small and close set, relative to head size.

Sus scrofa has an advanced sense of taste and a very good sense of smell. Long-range eyesight is poor. Interbreeding between feral and true wild pigs has led to a variety of ear shapes, ranging from small and erect to large and folded over at their fronts. Most prominent is the flat disk-shaped snout of tough cartilage, used for rooting in soil.

Although considered an omnivore, pigs have canines that might classify them as carnivores. The upper canines grow out to curve backward into large, arced tusks that function as tools for digging and as weapons. Tusk lengths range from 3 to 9 inches, with longer tusks indicating older animals. Upper and lower canines grow throughout the animal's life but are so closely set that jaw movements keep them honed to sharp points. (Canines are sometimes removed from farm piglets, but second-generation feral hogs have all of their natural teeth and tusks.)

Tail: The average length of the tail is about 8 inches. True wild boars have straight tails with tufted ends, while domestic swine tend to have coiled tails; hybrids may have a combination of both.

Tracks: Pigs are cloven-hooved with dewclaws usually printing to the rear of hoof prints. Tracks are equally sized, 2 to 4 inches long, shaped like deep U's. Dewclaws in front tracks are longer and more prominent than hind dewclaws.

Scat: Scat is usually large pellets, similar to those of a deer, but ranging from 3 to more than 6 inches long, sometimes massed together. When the animals have been feeding on succulent vegetation or rich meat, scats may become soft and disk shaped, like small cow pies. Recognizable content includes undigested plant fibers, insect legs and carapaces, seeds, and small bones.

Coloration: True wild boars possess a grizzled dark brown coat with whitish guard hairs that are typically longer and shaggier than those of hybridized feral pigs. Feral pigs often exhibit the splotched skin pigmentation of domestic hogs.

Sign: Well-traveled trails are made by herds of foraging pigs. Rooted-up soil with grasses and roots neatly clipped free are made by the animals' sharply mated incisors.

Vocalizations: Pigs make grunting, oinking, and squealing noises when excited or threatened. Some researchers believe that *Sus scrofa* speaks a rudimentary language, but a scientific analysis still needs to be performed.

Life span: Pigs live about twenty years.

Diet

Swine are believed to represent a primitive condition of ungulates because they have a simple digestive system with a two-chambered stomach that processes tough plant fibers less efficiently than the stomachs of deer or cows. Pigs are omnivorous, with a diet that includes fungi, leaves, roots, bulbs, fruit, snails, insects, snakes, earthworms, rodents, eggs, and carrion. They use their tough snout, tusks, and forefeet to unearth food plants.

Sus scrofa's broad diet has enabled the species to survive in a variety of environments, from deserts to mountainous terrain, so long as winter snows are shallow enough to permit the short, heavy pigs to travel without foundering. Their omnivorous diet brings swine into direct competition with black bears, and both species have killed one another in territorial disputes. Wild pigs aren't the gluttons they are purported to be and are typically much leaner than farm-raised hogs. Being self-sufficient, they are more active than domestic pigs and subsist on a less-fatty diet. Like domestic swine, wild pigs are host to parasitic infections (trichinosis, cysticercosis, brucellosis) that are transmittable to humans who eat undercooked meat and who make contact with suid scats.

Mating Habits

Swine become sexually mature at eighteen months but grow until five or six years. They are herd animals, and only one dominant male (boar) is permitted to breed, so males are driven from the herd to run in bachelor herds or to establish their own domains at two or three years of age.

Mating season runs from mid-November to early January, peaking in December. The rut can be unnaturally violent, and large boars frequently inflict serious, even mortal wounds on one another while battling for possession of a harem that may number up to eight sows. Extra thick skin covering the chest, shoulders, and underbelly offers some protection against stab wounds, but fights are usually bloody. Sows are in estrus for three weeks and are willing to copulate for three days during that period. Females not impregnated then will probably come into estrus again before the mating season ends. In northern regions, where snows are deeper and winters longer, sows birth one litter per year; in warmer climates breeding may take place year-round.

Gestation lasts about four months, with litters of three to sixteen (five is average) piglets being born in April. Newborns are 6 to 8 inches long and have brown fur patterned with nine or ten paler longitudinal stripes on the back. Sows withdraw from their herds to a secluded, defendable grass- or leaf-lined nest

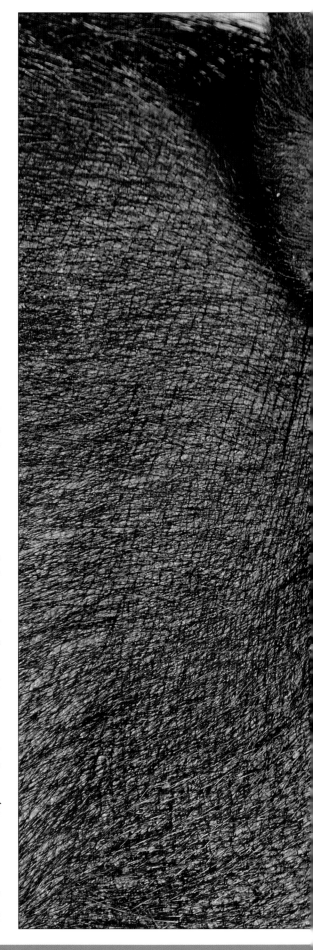

a day prior to giving birth. Few predators challenge a ferociously protective mother sow, but boars have been known to kill and eat their own newborns, while coyotes and birds of prey are quick to snatch piglets if they can. On average, only about half a litter can expect to reach maturity.

Sows rejoin their herd one to two days after giving birth, and by one week the small herd of mother and suckling young are able to travel with the larger extended-family herd. The young begin feeding on solid foods almost immediately but suckle from their mothers for three months. The piglets' stripes disappear entirely at about six months, and they take on the color and pattern that will mark them for life.

Behaviorisms

Wild *Sus scrofa* in Europe congregate in herds that may number 100 individuals, although twenty or fewer is normal. Sometimes two or more dominant females join their herds when food is abundant, finding greater safety in large numbers. Both sexes coexist peacefully, but in a defined hierarchy, at all times of year. Males eighteen months and older band together in bachelor herds or sometimes live alone during the nonbreeding months. Outsiders are challenged by dominant animals of either gender, particularly if food is scarce, but herd members are tolerant of one another.

Feral pigs are no more migratory than is necessary to find suitable habitat, but they can easily cover 10 miles a day. The normal gait is a trot of roughly 6 miles per hour, and pigs seldom walk except when feeding. At a fast run, the average adult can reach speeds in excess of 20 miles per hour.

In ancient times pigs served not only as food but also as farming tools: A plot of rough land could be made ready for arable crops just by turning a herd of pigs loose there, where the animals' natural rooting and pawing would loosen the soil as well as a drawn plow. Early Egyptians are said to have used deep swine hoof prints as planting holes for their seed, and pig dung is among the best fertilizers.

Sus scrofa's extremely acute sense of smell may be superior to that of a tracking dog, and it has long been exploited by humans to find truffles and other mushrooms of which pigs are fond. Pigs have been used experimentally for tracking people lost in a wilderness and for cadaver recovery, but the swine's temperament and lack of agility make this animal more difficult to work with than a dog. In medieval times pigs were trained to run down and kill game.

COLLARED PECCARY
(*Tayassu Tajacu*)

Peccaries are distant cousins of the African warthog and Eurasian wild boar but are smaller than true swine. Peccaries have fewer teeth than true swine and a two-chambered stomach that appears to be in transition between ruminants (cud chewers) and omnivores. There are two major species: the collared peccary and the white-lipped peccary, with fourteen recognized subspecies in North and South America.

Geographic Range

Collared peccaries are found in warmer latitudes, from northern Argentina throughout Central America and northward to Arizona, New Mexico, and Texas.

Habitat

In South and Central America, collared peccaries inhabit tropical rainforests and low mountain forests. In the southwestern United States and northern Mexico, the preferred habitat includes rocky deserts of saguaro, mesquite, and prickly pear cactus, which the pigs ingest, spines and all, with impunity. Collared peccaries are sometimes pests in residential areas, where they've become accustomed to rooting through human garbage.

Physical Characteristics

Mass: Collared peccaries weigh from 30 to 65 pounds.

True swine are not native to the Americas, but peccaries are found from southern North America to South America. (Photo courtesy Arizona Game and Fish.)

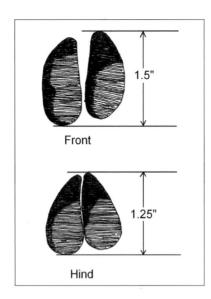

The cloven hooves of a peccary more closely resemble those of a deer than the more closely related wild boar.

Front

1.5"

Hind

1.25"

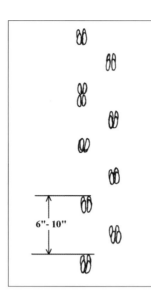

6"- 10"

Like wild pigs, peccaries, or javelina, tend to travel everywhere at a trot.

Body: The body is piglike, but much smaller than true swine, and stout and barrel shaped with short legs. Shoulder height is 20 to 22 inches; body length is 35 to 40 inches. The large head has a long, tapered muzzle, ending in a disk-shaped snout designed for rooting. Collared peccaries have short, straight tusks that fit together tightly enough to hone one another with every jaw movement, giving the species its common name, javelina (javelin-like). Javelinas have a distinct dorsal, or "precaudal," gland on the rump that secretes hormonal scents used in communication. Peccaries have poor eyesight, good hearing, and a rudimentary language.

Tail: The tail is about 3 inches long and straight, as a wild boar's.

Tracks: Peccaries have cloven hooves on all four feet, and tracks are 1 to 1.5 inches long. Stride is 6 to 10 inches; hind hooves usually register in front tracks. Peccaries have two dew-claws on the forefeet, one on the hind feet; true swine have two dewclaws on all four feet.

Scat: Scat is usually pellet-shaped segments, like those of deer, but much longer (2 to 3 inches). When peccaries are feeding on succulents, scats may be a flattened disk (cow-pie) shape. Scat may contain bones of rodents or birds, eggshells, and insect carapaces.

Long, spear-like canines show why early Spanish settlers called the peccary "javelina." (Photo courtesy Arizona Game and Fish.)

An icon of the American southwest, the peccary, or javalina, has been an important source of meat, of tough hides for shoes, and a source of revenue from sport hunters. (Photo courtesy Arizona Game and Fish.)

Peccary scat showing the little pig's fondness for eating prickly pear cactus—spines and all.

Coloration: The peccary's coarse hair is grizzled gray to nearly black with white guard hairs that give it a salt-and-pepper appearance. There is a yellowish patch on the cheeks and a collar of yellowish hair encircling the neck just ahead of the shoulders. Both genders are nearly identical in size and color, but male genitalia may be obvious.

Sign: Easily followed trails are made by a number of hooves and rooting noses. Chewed cactus, especially prickly pear leaves (spines and all are eaten), is a sure sign of peccaries. From downwind at closer ranges, there may be a scent of musk from the animals' urine and precaudal scent glands.

Vocalizations: Peccaries are grunts, squeals, and growls. Peccaries are very vocal, possibly because they possess poor long-distance vision and need to communicate vocally to keep contact with other herd members in sagebrush country, where visibility might be limited to a few feet. The alarm call is a coughing sound, almost a bark. Peccaries can squeal like pigs and do so when in mortal danger.

Life span: They can live fifteen to twenty years, up to twenty-four years in captivity.

Diet

Collared peccaries are herbivorous, with two stomachs for digesting coarse plant material, but they aren't picky eaters. Prickly pear cactus leaves are a legendary peccary food in arid regions, and peccaries will eat carrion given an opportunity. The species also eats frogs, snakes, lizards, the eggs of ground-nesting birds, roots, fungi, and fruits.

Mating Habits

Male collared peccaries reach sexual maturity at eleven months, females at eight months. There is no set mating season; rutting is triggered by changes in climate, particularly rain, to ensure that pregnancy and rearing of young occur during a plentiful season. Rain brings abundant food, which helps to guarantee that pregnant mothers are well fed, so most young are born in rainy months. Conversely, years of drought retard population growth.

As herd animals, peccaries live by a rigid social hierarchy. The dominant boar is the only male permitted to breed. Nonbreeding males may remain with the herd when rutting begins but are not allowed to approach females in estrus. Bachelor herds don't exist as they do in most herd species.

After a four-month gestation, mothers give birth to two to four piglets, with twins being the norm. In contrast to other social species that are predominantly female, the ratio between genders is approximately equal. Prior to giving birth, peccary mothers-to-be seek out a protected cave or other shelter in which to have their litters. Newborns are sometimes killed, possibly eaten, by more dominant herd members, especially if food is scarce. But that risk

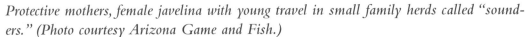

Protective mothers, female javelina with young travel in small family herds called "sounders." (Photo courtesy Arizona Game and Fish.)

passes quickly, and after one day, the mother and litter rejoin the herd, where she provides fierce protection for her offspring.

Peccary young are light brown with five wide black stripes running longitudinally down the back. They follow their mother everywhere but may be nursed by grown sisters from previous litters. Females have four nipples, but only the rear pair produce milk, forcing mothers to nurse while standing and the piglets to suckle from behind her, rather than from the side like true swine. Piglets begin feeding on vegetation within a week but are not weaned until two to three months.

Behaviorisms

Collared peccaries live in groups of five to fifteen individuals of all ages and both genders who eat, sleep, and forage together. A dominant boar leads, with subordinates ranked according to social prominence. Exceptions are the old, ill, and seriously injured, which are left behind when they can no longer keep pace.

Peccary herds avoid contact with groups outside their own territory and defend their territories against intruders. Feeding subgroups of males, females, and young form from within large herds, and these may break away to become the nucleus of new group herds. Territory size depends on herd numbers and the availability of food and water. Territorial boundaries are established by herd leaders, who employ urine, scats, and powerful-smelling oily musk glands to leave their scent on trees and other landmarks. Scats mark trail intersections and are refreshed periodically (usually daily). Herd members who meet after having been apart rub against one another head-to-rump, sharing spoor from scent glands.

Both peccary genders vigorously defend their young and their territory. Warning behaviors include laying back the ears, raising hair (hackles) along the spine, and releasing odorous musk from the rump (precaudal) gland. Next comes a pawing of the ground and an audible chattering of teeth. Finally, a peccary will charge, attempting to knock the adversary down, biting with canines, and sometimes locking jaws with an opponent. Fights may be bloody but are seldom more than superficially injurious before the weaker animal withdraws.

Collared peccaries are responsive to environmental changes, including precipitation, ambient temperatures, and length of day. Even feeding behavior changes with the seasons. When winter makes the desert cooler and the nights longer, foraging begins earlier in the evening and ends later in the morning. In summer, when days are hotter and longer, herds seek shade to sleep through the heat of the day, foraging only at night.

Considered a game animal, especially in Arizona, peccaries become nuisances by rooting up gardens or raiding trash cans. Their major predators—coyotes, pumas, jaguars, and bobcats—avoid human habitation, helping to explain the peccary's attraction to civilization. The species is not in danger, although about 20,000 are killed in Texas each year by sport hunters. Subspecies living in South America are threatened by rainforest destruction and loss of habitat.

Chapter 10

Pawed Animals

Family Canidae

Members of the dog family are characterized by having four toes on each paw (discounting a dewclaw that doesn't show in tracks), and each toe tipped with a fixed claw. A long tail is universal, as are long canine teeth designed for inflicting mortal wounds to prey. All are digitigrade, normally walking weight forward on the toes and prepared to instantly spring into pursuit or flight, so the heaviest impressions will be from toes and claws, with heel pads printing more faintly. All eat meat but also require vegetation in their diets. Every species has erect pointed ears that rotate to hone in on sounds, and all have an acute sense of smell.

Wolves and coyotes are social, living in family packs that might comprise several generations of offspring, with a dominant alpha (parent) pair who are the only members permitted to mate. Foxes are solitary except for mating. Adult males universally cock a leg to urinate against a usually stationary object to mark territory. Females squat to urinate, as do males in the presence of a dominant male, but ruling females may lift one foot slightly off the ground. Urine carries odors that identify individuals, territorial boundaries, gender, sexual readiness, size, and age.

Urine posts are refreshed, usually daily, and trackers should be mindful that scent posts often mark the boundaries between two territories.

GRAY WOLF
(*Canis lupus*)

The gray (or timber) wolf is the largest of forty-one species of wild canids worldwide. Gray wolves are the ancestors of all domestic dogs, including feral breeds such as Australian dingos (*Canis lupus dingo*) and New Guinea singing dogs (*Canis lupus halstromi*). Genetic evidence indicates that gray wolves were domesticated by humans at least twice, possibly as many as five times. All wolves in North America—except the red wolf (*Canis rufus*)—are *Canis lupus*, although some biologists split these into as many as thirty-two regional subspecies.

Long, strong legs, big feet for running more than 35 mph on snow and uneven terrain, sharp vision in daylight and darkness, keen hearing and sense of smell, the most massive and powerful jaws in the canid world, and a tail that never curls; all of these help to explain why tribes of old knew the gray wolf as "God's Knife."

Geographic Range

Gray wolves once occupied the northern hemisphere from the Arctic through central Mexico, North Africa, Europe, and Asia. Today there are an estimated 5,700 wolves living in the lower forty-eight United States, with approximately 4,000 of those in the Great Lakes region and about 1,500 in the northern Rocky Mountains. Canada claims an estimated 50,000 wolves, while Alaska estimates about 10,000; both classify wolves as game animals. In 2009, wolves in the Eastern Management Region of Michigan, Wisconsin, and Minnesota were removed from the endangered species list.

Once common throughout Europe, wolves are now scattered in Russia, Poland, Scandinavia, Spain, Portugal, and Italy, with small populations in Japan and Mexico. Wolves were exterminated from Great Britain in the 16th century and nearly so in Greenland during the 20th century. Today Greenland's wolves have recovered. The species has also shown resilience against advancing civilization in the United States, even expanding their range across Michigan's Mackinac Straits in 1997 to become established in the state's Lower Peninsula.

Habitat

Gray wolves are highly adaptable, able to live in most environments. A pack's territory may encompass hundreds of

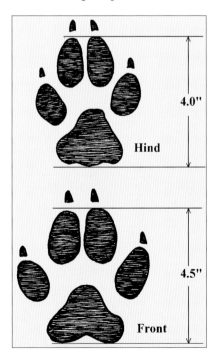

Gray wolf tracks.

4.0"

Hind

4.5"

Front

Biologists claim that each wolf accounts for twenty-seven deer per year, but that estimate doesn't take into account that a lone wolf can rarely catch a deer but can subsist entirely on small rodents and other animals—even fish.

square miles, but wolves range only as far as environmental factors demand. If an area provides prey and water without competition from other large predators, a territory may be only a few square miles. Where a pack's food supply is migratory, as with caribou herds on the Arctic tundra, packs may travel hundreds of miles. Studies show that road development has little effect on gray wolf migrations.

Physical Characteristics

Mass: Wolves weigh from 60 to 135 pounds; females are about 10 percent smaller.

Body: Wolves are doglike but with a more massive head and muzzle and heavier, longer legs. Body length is 40 to 50 inches; shoulder height is 26 to 38 inches. The normal gait is a trot of about 6 miles per hour that keeps the spine very straight, making an opportunistic wolf less noticeable than a dog with a typical rocking gait.

Tail: The tail is 14 to 20 inches long, bushy, darker on top than below, with a black or white tip. A gray wolf's tail never curls but is held straight down when relaxed, straight back when running, or straight up when agitated. All dogs, including wolf hybrids, curl their tails.

Tracks: Wolves have the largest tracks of all canids. The front is 4 to 5 inches long; the hind is 3.5 to more than 4 inches long. Tracks always show

An almost common occurrence; this adult blue heron was grabbed at night while it roosted in a marsh—note the outline of punctures in the shape of a wolf's jaw—but the young wolf that killed it hadn't yet learned that herons (unlike the tastier sandhill cranes) have a foul fishy taste.

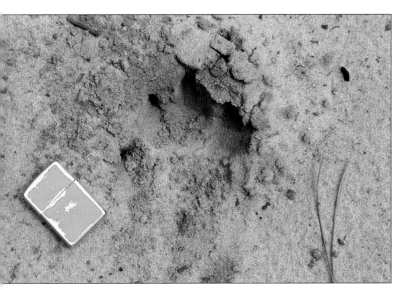

This wolf was alert—or "on its toes"—when it made this track. The heaviest toe impression on the right side indicates that this is a right-side paw print.

claws. Straddle is 4 to 6 inches; stride is 26 to 30 inches. Tracks are notably different from a coyote's and distinguishable from domestic dog tracks by their larger size and configuration. Hind heel pads have three distinct lobes to the rear—typical of canines—but front heel pads show only two lobes in tracks, leaving a chevron imprint that is unlike the three-lobed front tracks of a coyote or fox. Some dogs, like Siberian and malamute huskies, display a chevron-shaped fore track, but the tracks are smaller. Large feet distribute body weight over a wider area, like a snowshoe; the front track of a 90-pound yearling measures 4 inches long, while a dog of the same weight will have a front paw that measures 3.5 inches or less. Coyotes are sometimes mistaken for gray wolves, especially in their thick winter pelage, but a wolf is at least twice the size of its cousin, with a broader, less-pointed muzzle and shorter, less-pointed ears.

Scat: Scat is irregularly cylindrical, segmented, normally tapered at both ends, typically 1.5 to 2 inches in diameter, 6 to 8 inches long. Fur is wrapped in a spiral around the outside, encasing sharp bones that could harm the digestive tract. Fresher scats are dark brown or black, becoming gray as organic matter decomposes. Except for size, gray wolf scat is identical to other wild canids that share similar diets. One difference is that an adult wolf has bite pressure exceeding a half-ton per square inch, and it can crush larger bones to obtain fat-rich marrow, making large shards of bone a hallmark of wolf scat.

Coloration: Gray wolves tend to exhibit three color phases: The common gray phase is typified by combinations of coarser white guard hairs, with black, gray, red, and brown on the upper body and head. The back has a black saddle; the belly is lighter gray to white, with a black spot above the tail (precaudal) gland. Pups are normally born black, becoming grayer with age; black and darkly marked wolves are younger than lighter wolves. Completely white coats are most often seen on Arctic subspecies in the far north.

Sign: Gray wolves excavate burrows to capture marmots, but look for tracks, as bears, coyotes, and badgers also dig up marmots. Dominant males urinate on trees as territorial

The skull of this two-year-old female wolf shows the powerfully constructed jaw, heavy canines, and massive carnassial (cutting) molars that make the species such capable carnivores.

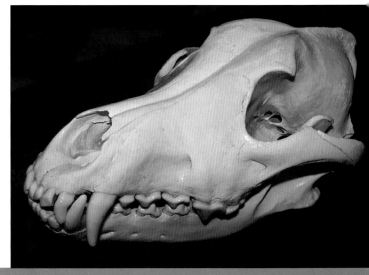

claims and an indication of social status. They urinate as high up on a tree as possible to demonstrate their size. Females may also urinate at scent posts, usually squatting, sometimes raising one leg. Wolves habitually transport large prey in pieces to a safe, often elevated, location before feeding. Regular feeding spots will be littered with bones.

Vocalizations: Wolves are normally silent, but a social lifestyle demands communication. Howling, heard most often at dusk when packs gather to hunt, is usually initiated by the alpha male. Gathering howls warn other packs that a territory is claimed and serves to get pack members psyched up for the hunt. Howls are mostly monotonal, occasionally wavering, but never with the yipping or prolonged barking of coyotes and dogs. Wolves issue a single, deep bark when alarmed but seem incapable of barking repeatedly.

Life span: Wolves live about ten years in the wild; up to fifteen years in captivity.

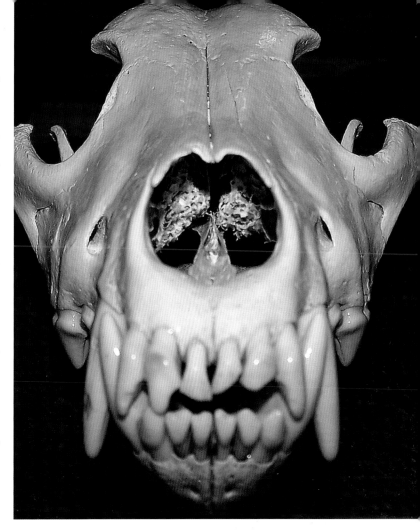

The chipped and worn incisors on this four-year-old gray wolf skull are an indication of how tough it is to live in the wild.

Diet

Gray wolves are meat eaters but require some vegetables to obtain minerals and vitamins not provided by prey. Wolves in captivity are usually fond of green beans; wild wolves eat blueberries, fruits, young grasses, and pine buds.

Renowned for the drill-team precision with which hunting packs bring down large quarry, wolves avoid prey that could injure one of them. The ideal prey is a weak, sickly individual, but deer that are weak from starvation are not eaten, because toxins accumulate in muscle mass when it cannibalizes itself.

In midwinter, when the alpha pair leaves to mate and seek out a den, packs may regroup at night to hunt larger prey. Mature pack members may strike out to find their own mates and territories. Lone wolves can rarely bring down deer, so much of their diet is mice, squirrels, rabbits, raccoons, and other small animals.

Mating Habits

Gray wolves mate between January and March, with those in the southern latitudes breeding first because spring comes to them earlier. Only the parent, or alpha, pair mate within a pack, which is itself a family unit. Adult offspring naturally leave to establish their own ter-

The left front track of a 140-pound gray, or "timber," wolf. Like nearly all quadrupeds, the largest, most heavily imprinted toe is the outermost, opposite the human design.

ritories at two to four years of age, but weaker omega wolves may remain with the parents indefinitely.

Like other canids, a female wolf's breeding cycle has four stages: anestrus, proestrus, estrus, and diestrus. Estrus (when the female can copulate) lasts five to fourteen days, half that of a dog. Males are brought into heat by females; their testicles, which are normally retracted, unlike dogs', descend only during this period.

Two weeks prior to mating, the alpha pair leaves the pack to dig a den, always near a source of freshwater. Dens begin with a tunnel, roughly 18 inches in diameter and 10 feet long. The tunnel opens into a chamber about 4 feet high by 6 feet long and 6 feet wide, with an elevated floor to prevent flooding. Small caves and natural shelters may be used, so long as these offer protection from the elements and predators (bears) that eat pups. The same den may be used every year if it is left unmolested.

As the pregnant alpha female becomes more vulnerable, she will spend more time in the den, and her mate will bring her food. Gestation lasts sixty days, with pups born between March and May, depending on how long winter lasts in that region. Litter size is typically six, with newborn pups weighing eight ounces.

Born blind and deaf, newborn pups are completely dependent on their mother for eight weeks; she will stay with them constantly, except to drink and expel waste, for their first three weeks. During this time she will also make sure that the den's interior is fastidiously cleaned of anything that might bring disease to her young. Pups gain about three pounds per week, feeding on rich milk and regurgitated meat. Predigested meat is easier for the young pups to metabolize, and adults can carry more of it in their stomachs than in their mouths.

Pups are weaned at nine weeks, freeing the mother to join pack mates on hunts. Pups leave the den to play fight, watched over by a babysitter (usually the weakest member of the pack). By ten months, the pups have grown to 65 pounds and hunt with the pack. Female pups are sexually mature at two years and may leave to find their own mates. Males reach full maturity at three years.

Behaviorisms

Gray wolves are exceptionally social, with pack sizes ranging from two recently mated animals to more than thirty. A pack is actually a family, usually the alpha pair and their offspring and sometimes a brother or sister of the alphas. Unrelated adults are rarely accepted into an existing pack, but orphaned pups are always adopted.

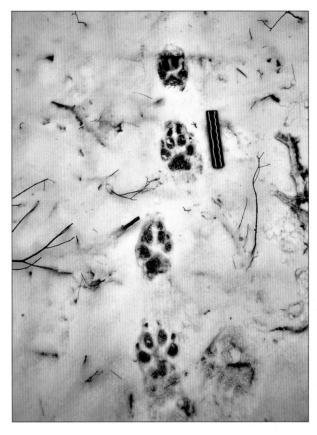

Gray wolf track pattern in fresh snow. Bottom to top: Left front, left hind, right front, right hind.

Wolf packs must have a hierarchy: Alpha males lead, but packs have been ruled by a widowed alpha female. Pack members are subordinate to the alphas. If an alpha male is killed, the female may leave to seek out a new mate, leaving the beta, or second strongest male, to lead. Newly paired alpha mates seeking their own domains may travel with a third female, usually a sister of the alpha female. This ensures that a mated pair has the strength to take large prey and provides a backup mate should the original alpha female be killed. The second female also serves as a babysitter for the first litter of pups.

Packs virtually never fight among themselves, because harming a member of the team weakens its ability to hunt. The pack hierarchy is strictly adhered to: Alphas and pups eat first, followed by betas, subordinates, down to the omega (or lowest-ranking) wolf. Pack members are brought food if they become incapacitated, but they often leave the pack voluntarily.

Wolf packs have two annual phases: The stationary phase occurs during spring and summer, when pups are too small to travel with the pack. The nomadic phase spans from autumn to late winter, when packs follow migratory or yarded deer herds. A pack may travel more than 75 miles in a day, most of it at night, at a lope of about 15 miles per hour.

The track pattern of a walking coyote (bottom) contrasts with the red fox track pattern above. The coyote front track is 3 inches, while the fox tracks are 1.5 inches. Note the "mustache" at rear of the coyote's front heel pad, and that the hind foot registers on top of the front track.

COYOTE
(*Canis latrans*)

This miniature wolf takes its name from the Nahuatl tribe, who called it *coyotl* (the "trickster"). All tribes within its range respected the species for its intelligence. With the extermination of large predators, coyotes became the dominant carnivore in North America, and the species has thrived in every environment, from desert and forest to prairie and suburb.

Geographic Range

Native to the Americas, coyotes are found from Central America throughout Mexico and the lower forty-eight states, northward into central Canada and Alaska.

Habitat

Coyotes have proved very adaptable to a broad range of environments and climates. They thrive in the southern Mexico jungles, the deserts of the Southwest, and in bitter-cold northern forests. Coyotes in many areas have learned to recognize people as a food source, and in suburban areas they have made themselves pests by raiding garbage cans.

Physical Characteristics

Mass: Coyotes weigh from 30 to more than 60 pounds in the far north.

Body: Coyotes are lanky and more slender than the gray wolf. Body length is 40 to 50 inches; shoulder height is 23 to 26 inches. They have large pointed ears and a narrow tapered muzzle, with small black nose pad. The coyote is about half the size of a gray wolf and much larger than any fox. The eyes have a yellow iris and round pupil. Molars are structured for crushing small bones, and canines are long and narrow.

Tail: The tail is roughly half the body length, 20 to 25 inches long, bushy with a black tip. A coyote's tail droops normally and is held below the back when running, while a gray wolf's tail is nearly always held straight back, in line with the spine.

Tracks: Tracks are about 2.5 inches long for the forepaws, and hind paws are roughly 10 percent smaller. Tracks as long as 3.5 inches have been reported in northern forests. Heel pads of all four feet have three rearward lobes. Walking stride is 14 inches, straddle is 4 inches.

Scat: Scat is black to brown, growing lighter and grayer with age; length is 3 to more than 4 inches, cylindrical, segmented, about 1 inch in diameter. May be a purplish color in blueberry season, but it is usually wrapped in a sheath of fur that encases small bones and indigestible objects.

Coloration: Fur is gray-brown to yellow-gray, often with rust-colored patches around the neck, shoulders, and flanks and usually grizzled black on the back. Belly and throat are lighter, even cream colored. Forelegs, sides of the head, muzzle, and feet are reddish brown. There is one molt per year, beginning with profuse shedding in May and ending in July. Winter coats grow in late August or in September in more southerly ranges.

Arguably the most successful and adaptable carnivore in the Americas, Canis latrans *ranges from the Arctic Circle to Central America.*

A coyote that scratches with all four feet after urinating is advertising its claim to the surrounding territory.

Sign: Sign includes urine-scented tree trunks and stumps, marked by males about 8 inches above the ground, or half as high up as a gray wolf, and gnawed rib ends and cartilaginous joints on deer carcasses. Large leg bones are left intact, not crushed as they would be by a wolf or bear.

Vocalizations: Coyotes make shrill howling, barking, and yapping noises, almost screeching at times, especially when family members congregate at dusk or dawn. The scientific name, *Canis latrans*, is Latin for "barking dog."

Life span: They live eight to ten years.

Diet

Coyotes are mostly carnivorous, eating almost any type of meat: lizards, snakes, grasshoppers, birds, eggs, even fish. An average diet consists of squirrels, rabbits, and especially mice. One of nature's best mousers, coyotes stand motionless in the middle of a meadow, cocking their heads and ears from one position to another as they pinpoint the location of scurrying rodents under grass or snow. When a mouse has been located, the coyote leaps into the air, often clearing the ground with all four feet, and pounces onto its prey with the forefeet. This technique is effective in winter, when rodents travel under snow through tunnels that a coyote can collapse by jumping onto them, trapping prey inside. Once caught, rodents are swallowed whole.

Coyotes are often seen by hunters who bait deer, because the little wolves have learned to associate hunters with both vegetables and fresh meat. In winter, coyote families may form a pack to hunt small, weakened deer, but they prefer safer prey like rabbits and voles. Deer are large and dangerous to even a pack of coyotes, whose members are one-third the size of an adult whitetail. A sharp-hooved kick to the ribs or jaw could be fatal if it prevents a coyote from eating or running fast, so deer are low on the coyote's list of preferred prey, and those they do hunt will be weak or wounded.

Coyotes are fond of fruits, including blueberries, wild grapes, elderberries, and other sugar-rich fruits that help to put on precious fat against the cold of winter. In blueberry country the scat of coyotes, and all canids, will frequently be purple between the months of August and October.

Mating Habits

Both genders reach sexual maturity at twelve months but, to prevent inbreeding, must leave their parents' territory to find mates. Mated pairs are monogamous but infrequently "divorce" to take other mates, even after being together for several years.

Coyote pairs retire to a secluded den in January, using the same site year after year if it remains unmolested. Dens are excavated near water, sometimes under the roots of a large tree, and always in a place where good drainage keeps the den from flooding during wet weather. Each den is a smaller version of a wolf den, consisting of a narrow tunnel about 12 inches in diameter that extends up to 10 feet, terminating at a nursing chamber that measures 3 feet high, 3 feet wide, and 4 feet long.

Mating season is late January through March. Copulation is usually initiated by the female, who paws at the male's flanks to indicate her estrus. Females are monoestrous, remaining in heat for just five days, so there is urgency to become pregnant. Like those of a wolf, a male coyote's testicles remain retracted until mating season prompts them to descend.

Actual coitus between coyote pairs occurs between February and March. Gestation is sixty days, with a litter of one to as many as nineteen pups born in April or May. Pups weigh seven ounces at birth. At ten days pups will have doubled in size, and their eyes will have opened. At three to four weeks, the pups emerge from the den to play while parents protect them from birds of prey, especially. The male brings food to his family, feeding pups regurgitated meat and occasionally

Typical coyote scat at a trail intersection serves as a territorial marker. Note feather quill between 3- and 4-inch marks, and an abundance of fine rodent hairs.

This well-run trail along the sloping bank of a river allows coyotes to patrol silently while looking for prey below, yet able to see into the surrounding forest without revealing more than its own head.

babysitting while the mother leaves to drink or relieve herself. At thirty-five days the pups weigh three to four pounds and are weaned.

Coyote pups mature quickly; by six months they weigh nearly thirty pounds and can fend for themselves. By nine months, male pups typically strike out on their own, while female pups may remain—babysitters for future generations—for about two years.

The coyote is a genetically unique species but shows a penchant for interbreeding with similar canids. The red wolf (*Canis rufus*) is thought to be disappearing as a species partly because it breeds readily with coyotes. Dogs, particularly those with coyote-like characteristics, have also mated with coyotes, producing a hard-to-identify "coydog." Most recently, DNA testing has revealed that probably most of the gray wolves in Minnesota have some coyote genes in their bloodlines.

Behaviorisms

Because coyotes are so well equipped to catch small prey, they seldom form packs. Packs that do exist form up at dusk, gathered by prolonged howls from the alpha male, who is greeted by high-pitched yaps and barks from those (mostly offspring) that join him. Pack members may split up while hunting, communicating the find of meals large enough to be shared with long, broken howls that are much higher pitched than the monotonal howls of the gray wolf. Nightly hunts encompass roughly 3 square miles.

Coyote territories are only as large as required but generally encompass less than 12 square miles. Territories are bounded by olfactory scent posts consisting of urine and scat deposits left on trails, especially at intersections. Most scent marking is done by males, but alpha females may also scent territories.

Right front foot of a 50-pound coyote on packed early-spring sand; smallest innermost toes failed to print clearly, while larger innermost toes pressed hard into the sand.

Coyote walking track pattern in wet sand. Hind foot registers ahead of front foot—not uncommon.

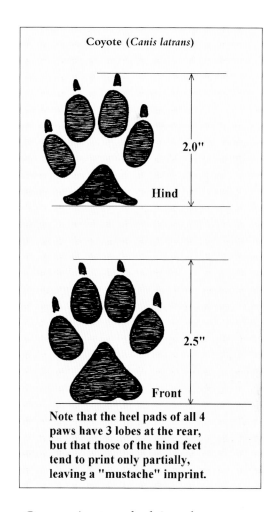

Coyote (*Canis latrans*)

2.0"

Hind

2.5"

Front

Note that the heel pads of all 4 paws have 3 lobes at the rear, but that those of the hind feet tend to print only partially, leaving a "mustache" imprint.

One ancient myth claims that coyotes and badgers (*Taxidea taxus*) sometimes hunt together cooperatively, the coyote using its acute nose to locate burrowed rodents, which the badger digs out. Badger and coyote do double-team burrowed prey, but the badger's keen nose needs no assistance, and the two do not share meals. The intelligent coyote knows to position itself near the escape tunnels common to burrowing species, waiting while the single-minded badger digs toward its prey. The cornered prey can wait for certain death from the badger, or it can try popping out of an escape tunnel, risking the coyote's lightning-fast jaws.

GRAY FOX
(*Urocyon cinereoargenteus*)

North America's largest native fox, the gray has never been as visible as its imported European cousin, the red fox. (Photo courtesy National Parks Service.)

Gray foxes are native to North America and were in fact the reason that red foxes were imported to the New World from Europe. When early settlers attempted to practice the nobleman's sport of fox hunting from horseback, they learned that this continent's largest native fox has a unique ability to extend its semi-retractable claws and climb trees like a cat. In the vast forests of America, this made for a short chase, so the non-climbing red fox was imported for sporting purposes.

Geographic Range

Gray foxes range from southern Canada to northern Venezuela and Colombia. This species does not inhabit the more-mountainous areas of the northwestern United States, the Great Plains, deserts, or eastern Central America.

Habitat

Gray foxes inhabit forests where their unique ability to climb trees allows them to escape predators. They may be seen in adjoining fields where they forage for grasshoppers and rodents, but they are never very far from tall trees.

Physical Characteristics

Mass: Gray foxes weigh 7 to 13 pounds.

Body: They have a long bushy tail, short legs, and elongated body; body length is 31 to 44 inches, shoulder height is about 14 inches. The broad skull with widely spaced temporal ridges distinguishes it from other North American canids. The muzzle is narrow and tapered, ending in a small black nose pad. Ears are shorter and less pointed than those of the red fox. Males are only slightly larger than females.

Tail: The tail is bushy, black-tipped, 8 to 17 inches long, and typically shorter than the red fox's.

Tracks: Tracks are about 1.5 inches long for all four feet, hind foot slightly narrower than front. Semi-retractable claws usually show in tracks. Heel pads of front and hind feet have three rearward-pointed lobes, but usually only the outer edges of the outermost lobes show in hind tracks.

Scat: Scat is segmented, tapered at one or both ends, 2.5 inches long, 0.5 inch in diameter, and often encased in a spiral of fine rodent fur. It is indistinguishable from red fox scat, except that gray foxes normally eat a more-vegetarian diet of berries and fruits, and their scats contain more seeds and vegetable matter.

Coloration: It is easily confused with a red fox, especially when the latter is a "cross" phase of mottled red, gray, and black fur. The gray fox is grizzled gray and black along its back, neck, and upper tail. The upper head and muzzle are grizzled, with patches of white at the tip of the muzzle, on the cheeks, and on the underbelly. Sides of the neck, legs, body, and tail are rust-colored.

The gray fox's semi-retractable claws give it a unique ability to scale trees. (Photo courtesy Illinois Dept. of Natural Resources.)

Gray fox scat in early autumn, showing a predominance of blueberries, a vital pre-winter staple for most carnivores.

Although classed as a carnivore, the gray fox diet is comprised largely of berries and insects, with a few rodents, crayfish, and other small animals. (Photo courtesy Berkeley University.)

Sign: Sign includes food caches buried in shallow holes or holes left by removing cached foods, trees that have been marked with urine at a height of about 8 inches, and yellow stains on snow. Gray foxes are unusual among wild canids because they tend to den throughout the year, typically under tree roots, in rock crevices, or in hollow trees, and individuals often have several dens within their territories. Den entrances are much smaller than those of coyotes, largely because coyotes prey on gray foxes.

Vocalizations: Gray foxes make high-pitched barks, yaps, and growls, like those of a small dog. They are less vocal than red foxes.

Life span: They live eight to ten years.

Diet

Gray foxes are good hunters, able to pounce on mice in fields or catch rabbits in brushy swamps, but this canid's diet has an added dimension because it can climb trees to snatch roosting birds at night or to rob nests of their eggs. They prey on frogs, grasshoppers, and locusts; eat carrion; and catch small fish.

Gray foxes also eat vegetation, probably more than any other wild canid. Blueberries are a favorite, but the gray fox can

Similar in size and general outline to the red fox, a gray fox's heel pads can often reveal its species in tracks.

Gray Fox track pattern

Walking

climb into the upper branches of fruiting trees, like wild cherries, to get fruits that are beyond the reach of its non-climbing cousins.

Mating Habits

Gray foxes become sexually mature at ten months. Mating occurs in late winter—March in the north, February in the south. (A rule of thumb is that gray foxes mate about one month after red foxes.) Mated pairs are believed to be monogamous.

Gestation is fifty days, with up to seven pups born in a secluded woodland den in April or May. Pups nurse for three months. The father brings food to the nursing mother and stands guard while she leaves to drink or relieve herself, but he takes no active role in parenting during the suckling stage and doesn't enter the den.

Gray fox pups are the most precocious of North American canids; immediately after weaning they leave the den and begin hunting with their parents. At four months, the pups have all of their permanent teeth and weigh about seven pounds. By five months the pups have left to fend for themselves, and the mates separate to resume a normally solitary lifestyle. Radio telemetry data indicate that separated family members remain within their own established territories, so inbreeding is unlikely.

Gray Fox tracks

2.0"

Front

1.5"

Hind

Heel pads of front and hind paws are 3-lobed, but outer lobes of hind feet tend to print only partially, with a mustache pattern.

Behaviorisms

Gray foxes are solitary deep-forest dwellers, and a tracker who sees one should count himself or herself lucky. The species is reclusive and seldom vocal, keeping to secluded dens in shadowed woods by day and hunting at night. This secretive behavior is explained by the fact that so many species, including raptors, coyotes, and bears, consider them prey.

But gray foxes are not easy prey; their light weight allows them to run across snow and boggy areas that are too soft to support larger carnivores. Sharp, semiretractable claws enable them to climb trees after sleeping squirrels and to escape enemies that they can't outrun. Gray foxes have been labeled as chicken killers, but instances where they have been guilty are rare. Most often the culprit is a raccoon, but such leaps of logic are made believable by adages like "a fox in the henhouse" and "sly as a fox."

RED FOX
(*Vulpes vulpes*)

Native to Europe, the red fox was transplanted into North America so that early noblemen could enjoy the gentleman's sport of fox hunting from horseback with hounds. The native gray fox, with its ability to climb trees, was unacceptable prey, so the red fox (which cannot climb trees) was brought to the New World. Soon after, the red fox, with its phenomenal adaptability to the most hostile environments, had escaped captivity to become permanently established as part of the American ecosystem.

Geographic Range

Red foxes have thrived in every location. Today the species is common throughout the continental United States; in all but the most frigid regions of Canada and Alaska, where it overlaps the range of the arctic fox; and in Australia, Japan, and across Asia.

Habitat

Red foxes occupy an extraordinary range of habitats that includes deciduous and pine forests, arctic tundra, open prairies, and farmland. The species has become common in suburban areas, where it preys on rodents more adroitly than a house cat. Preferred habitats have a diversity of plant life, particularly fruits and berries. Unlike the reclusive gray fox, red foxes are frequently seen in open places.

Physical Characteristics

Mass: Red foxes weigh 7 to 15 pounds.

Body: They have a slender, elongated body and short legs; body length is 35 to 40 inches; shoulder height is 15 inches. Ears are long and pointed, with black backside; muzzle is long and slender, tipped with a prominent black button nose. Eyes are yellow, denoting good night vision.

Tail: The tail is bushy, rust colored, and 13 to 17 inches long, with a white (sometimes black) tip. A precaudal scent gland is located on the dorsal base of the tail, identifiable by a patch of dark fur.

Tracks: Tracks are larger than those of the gray fox but with smaller toe pads. About 2.5 inches long, the hind foot slightly smaller and narrower. There are four toes on each foot, with claws showing. Feet are heavily furred in winter. Heel pads of all four feet leave a chevron-shaped print. A noticeable ridge runs across the front heel pad, also in a chevron shape, that prints more deeply than the rest of the pad.

Scat: Scat is similar to that of other canids—cylindrical, segmented, and tapered at the ends but with a predominance of berry seeds and vegetable matter when available. It often has a spiral of fur wrapped around small bones and is 0.5 inch in diameter by 4 inches long.

A nonnative immigrant that was purposely brought to America by settlers from the Old World, the red fox is a marvel of adaptability whose range extends from the Arctic Circle to Central America.

An adept hunter, the red fox is the marathon runner of foxes, able to chase down tree squirrels (shown) before they can climb to safety, and even to snatch flushed birds out of the air.

Coloration: Fur is rust colored to deep reddish brown on the upper parts, whitish on the underside. The lower part of the legs is usually black. There are two cross phases that sometimes occur: One, the "cross fox," is a grizzled coat of intermingled rust and black fur with a usually reddish belly; the other is the "silver fox" phase, with a silver-gray upper body and black mask around eyes, dark gray to black legs. Too common to be mutations, cross foxes make up about 25 percent of a given population, and silver foxes make up about 10 percent.

Sign: Spring birthing dens are excavated in the sides of hills, marked by a fan of loose soil around a main entrance that may measure 12 inches across. Escape tunnels branch from the underground chamber, usually within 10 feet of the main entrance. Small mounds or holes where food was cached nearby indicate an active den.

Vocalizations: They are more vocal than the gray fox, with high-pitched yapping and barking, reminiscent of a small dog. The alarm call is a single sharp, high-pitched bark, almost a shriek.

Life span: Red foxes live ten years.

Diet

Classified as a carnivore, this fox is almost omnivorous, eating rodents, rabbits, fish, and insects, as well as fruits. Blueberries are a favorite, but grapes, pears, apples, and most fruits are favored.

Red foxes are skilled rodent hunters. Like the coyote, a fox stands motionless in a meadow, cocking

Typical red fox scat, three-quarters of an inch in diameter, with segments joined together by a sheath of rodent fur, reveals a more carnivorous diet than the gray fox.

its head from one side to another, swiveling its acutely directional ears to pinpoint a mouse scurrying under grass or snow. When a mouse is located, the fox springs high into the air, all four feet leaving the ground, and comes down hard onto the rodent with both forefeet, stunning the prey.

Bolder than most wild canids, red foxes in autumn have learned to associate humans and gunshots with the rich venison liver, kidneys, and heart that some deer hunters leave behind.

Mating Habits

Mating season is timed with the arrival of warm weather, varying up to four months from one region to another. In the deep south, mating occurs in December and January; in central states, from January to February; in the far north, between late February and April.

Vixen (female) red foxes are in estrus for six days. Females signal their readiness to prospective mates through pheromonal scents several days prior to coming into heat. During the preheat period, males fight almost bloodlessly to compete for breeding status. Males have an annual cycle of "fecundity" (sperm production) and are sterile the rest of the year.

Copulation lasts about fifteen minutes, punctuated by barking and yapping from the male. Females may mate with more than one male to help ensure impregnation. Delayed implantation prevents fertilized eggs from attaching to the uterine wall for ten to fourteen days and helps to guarantee that a female is physically fit for pregnancy; if she isn't, the fertilized egg spontaneously aborts.

Red foxes lack the grizzled black saddle of the gray fox and have black legs. Bright yellow eyes denote good night vision.

Red Fox track patterns

Walk   Trot   Run

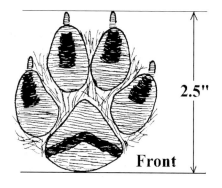

Red Fox tracks

2.5"

Front

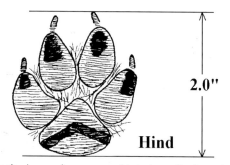

2.0"

Hind

Red fox tracks in mud or snow: Note heavily furred soles. Darker portions indicate deepest impressions; if visible, the raised chevron-shaped ridge on the fox's heel pads is a definite identifier.

Pregnant females pair off with their strongest mate, retiring to a secluded location to excavate a birthing den. The male doesn't enter the den after its completion. Gestation lasts forty-nine to fifty-six days, with shorter periods indicating healthier mothers.

Between February and May, depending on latitude, the female births five to thirteen kits (pups). Kits are born blind and weigh three ounces. By fourteen days their eyes are open, and at five weeks, pups are playing outside, running back into the den when the mother barks an alarm. Kits are weaned at ten weeks, and the father, who has provided food to mother and kits, leaves to resume a solitary life.

Kits remain with the mother, learning to hunt and forage, until the following autumn when the young adults disperse, sometimes traveling more than 100 miles before taking a mate at ten months of age.

Behaviorisms

Red foxes are solitary hunters of small animals. The prolific nature of rodents keeps the average territory small, as does an omnivorous diet of berries and fruits, but there will always be a source of water somewhere within a typical range of 3 to 9 square miles. Territorial battles are rare and are seldom more than a nip-and-chase, with the resident fox having the home advantage.

More nomadic than the gray fox, a red fox has several dens throughout its territorial range; these dens are linked to each other, and to buried food caches, by trails that are patrolled daily. One of these is a maternal den that will be used year after year, so long as it remains undisturbed. The others provide owners with a place to escape if chased by larger predators. With a remarkably fast running speed of 30 miles per hour, a healthy, alert fox can usually reach safety before being overtaken by a faster carnivore.

Red foxes are known to take an occasional chicken, but predation is limited to small animals, and very often foxes take the blame for the marauding of skunks and raccoons.

Family Felidae

Cats are a family of hunters that split off from other mammals during the Eocene Period, 40 million years ago. All are endowed with acute senses of smell, hearing, and vision and sensitive whiskers that can detect changes in air currents. All species are armed with very sharp retractable claws on all four of their toes, as well as a front dewclaw that functions like an opposable thumb to grip prey. Cats possess uncanny stealth, lightning-fast reflexes, daggerlike canines that kill quickly with a brain-piercing bite to the base of a victim's skull, and unmatched agility. Most hunt at night, when extraordinary night vision and binocular eyesight gives them an advantage over their prey. Cats may eat fresh carrion, but they don't normally eat animals that have been dead long enough to decay, the way scavenging coyotes and bears do.

JAGUAR
(*Panthera onca*)

Revered as a forest god by pre-Columbian civilizations in southern Mexico, Guatemala, and Peru, the jaguar's name means "kills in a single bound." There are eight subspecies, all threatened, and some are extinct except in zoos. The greatest threats to this largest American cat come from buyers of illegal furs, who pay exorbitant prices for the jaguar's spotted pelt, and the clearing of old-growth forest, where the cat's dappled coat provides good camouflage. Little is known about how jaguars live in the wild, and most existing data have been gathered from zoo specimens.

Like several species, including leopards, red foxes, and occasionally a cougar, individual jaguars may have a "black panther" coat. (Photo courtesy US Fish & Wildlife.)

Massive head, powerful build, and large feet make America's largest cat a formidable hunter. (Photo courtesy US Fish & Wildlife.)

Geographic Range

Native to Central America, jaguars once ranged as far north as Arizona, but by the late 1900s, none were thought to exist north of Mexico. Two independent sightings in 1996 confirmed jaguars still reached as far north as Arizona and New Mexico. In February 2009, the only known free-living jaguar in the United States was euthanized in Arizona after suffering kidney failure (common among old cats). Today most jaguars live in Argentina and Brazil and as far south as Patagonia.

Habitat

Typical jaguar habitat provides large prey and plenty of water, preferably in canopied forest where their spotted coats are hard to distinguish among undergrowth and dappled sunlight. Dense jungle and scrub forest, reed thickets along waterways, and shoreline forests are ideal, but the species has been seen in the rocky desert country favored by cougars.

Physical Characteristics

Mass: Males weigh 120 to 300 pounds, and females weigh 100 to 200 pounds.

Body: Jaguars are stout and larger and more stocky than a cougar, with a spotted coat, thick limbs, and a massive head. Body length is about 4 feet, shoulder height is 2.5 to 3 feet.

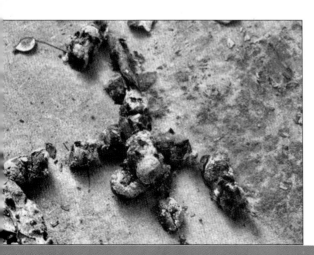

This jaguar scat, about a week old and turning white with age, is similar to that of other large predators, but will probably contain remnants of alligators and other aquatic animals. (Photo courtesy Kansas State University.)

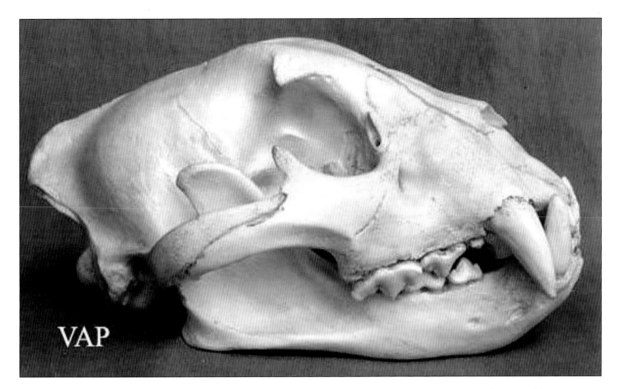

This reproduction jaguar skull shows the powerful jaws and very strong canines that enable it to quickly bring down large prey. (Photo courtesy of The Bone Room.)

Tail: The tail is 18 to 30 inches long, spotted with a black tip, and shorter and thinner than the mountain lion's.

Tracks: Forefoot is 4 to 4.5 inches, nearly as wide as it is long, leaving a print that is almost round. Hind prints are slightly smaller. Toes are much smaller and heel pads much larger than those of the mountain lion. Heel pads of all four feet are three lobed, but the two outermost lobes in a jaguar's front track are larger than the center lobe and extend more rearward, whereas the three lobes in a mountain lion's front track are of nearly equal size. Walking stride is 20 inches but may vary greatly in the cat's jungle habitat; straddle is 8 to 10 inches.

Scat: Scat is nearly identical to cougar scats; cylindrical, segmented, tapered at one or both ends, usually with fur wrapped around the scat in spiral fashion; about 5 inches long by 1.5 inches in diameter. Differences may be evident from the jaguar's tendency to prey on aquatic animals, including alligators and fish.

Coloration: Jaguars are normally yellow and tan with a mottling of black rings, many of which have a single black dot inside—a bull's-eye pattern. Cheeks, throat, underbelly, and insides of the legs are white. It isn't

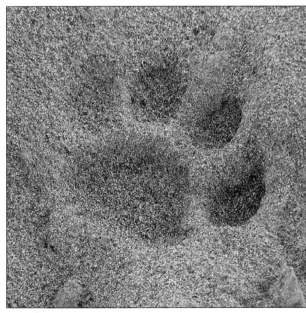

Left hind track of a jaguar in damp sand. (Photo courtesy US Fish & Wildlife.)

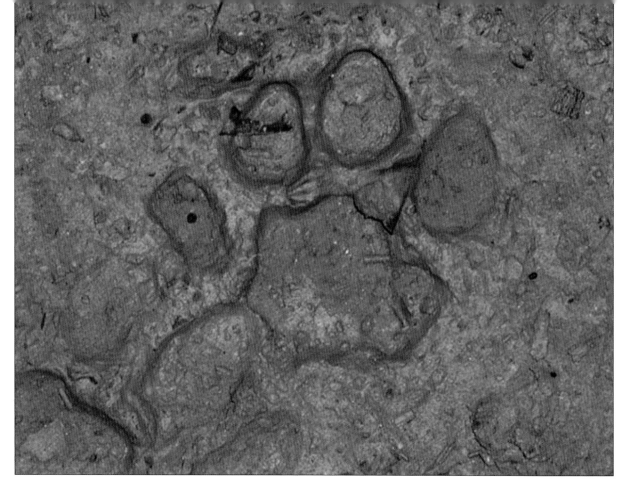

Right front paw print of a jaguar in mud shows why the cat is such a powerful swimmer. (Photo courtesy US Fish & Wildlife.)

uncommon for a jaguar to be black, a phase in which the cat is known as a black panther. Black panthers are spotted, but mottling is subdued by a coat that's nearly as dark as the spots.

Sign: Sign includes scat deposits at trail intersections, usually near trees that have been clawed and sprayed with urine; alligator remains near water; and large cat tracks on shorelines that enter or exit the water.

Vocalizations: Jaguars are the only New World cats that can roar. Roars differ from those of an African lion, being a series of loud coughs rather than a single unbroken roar.

Life span: Jaguars live up to twenty-two years in captivity; life span in the wild is unknown but probably fifteen years.

Diet

Panthera onca is very much a predator, feeding on terrestrial prey that includes deer, peccaries, and alpacas. The only wild felid that enjoys swimming, jaguars also take aquatic animals that include nutria (a larger cousin to the muskrat), fish, and alligators or caimans up to 5 feet long.

Mating Habits

Jaguars are sexually mature at three years. Females breed once every two years. Those in tropical regions may breed at any time of year, while those in the north generally mate in December or January. Females are monogamous, accepting a single mate per pregnancy.

The gestation period for jaguars is ninety-three to 110 days. Prior to giving birth, the mother, still accompanied by her mate, dens in a small rock cave, a hollow beneath the roots of a tree, or another secure and dry refuge. Jaguars are poor diggers, so dens are natural or appropriated from other animals.

Litter size is one to four cubs, born blind but furred, weighing 1.5 to 2 pounds each. The mother remains with the cubs constantly until weaning them at forty days, leaving the den only to relieve herself and drink while the father jaguar guards the den. While cubs are denned, the father jaguar brings food and guards the den but does not enter.

When cubs are two months old and able to travel with the mother, the parents separate; fathers take no role in rearing offspring. Cubs will be proficient hunters of small prey at six months but remain with the mother for another year before going on their own. Female cubs may remain with the mother for two years but must leave before she mates again.

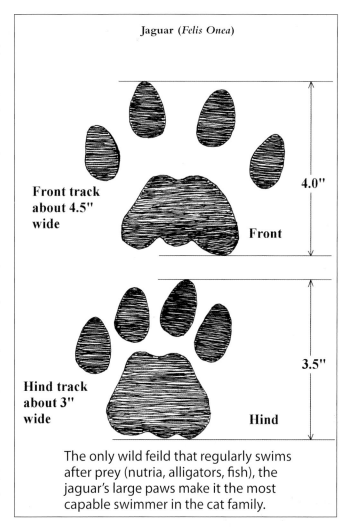

Jaguar (*Felis Onea*)

Front track about 4.5" wide

4.0"

Front

Hind track about 3" wide

3.5"

Hind

The only wild feild that regularly swims after prey (nutria, alligators, fish), the jaguar's large paws make it the most capable swimmer in the cat family.

Behaviorisms

Jaguars are solitary, interacting only during the mating period. The cats are known to live within a territorial radius of only 3 miles, but if food is scarce, they may roam 200 miles in search of more-suitable habitat. Jaguars are fast runners but only for short distances. They climb well, are excellent swimmers, and prefer habitats with abundant freshwater. A keystone species in tropical ecosystems, jaguar predation on herbivorous and granivorous mammals is crucial for controlling prolific species whose overpopulation can negatively impact native flora.

Jaguars have preyed on domestic animals, mostly as the result of clearing forest to move farms into the cats' habitat. Jaguars bear a reputation as man-eaters, but Miskito Indians tell stories of jaguars emerging from the forest to play with village children. Mayan tribes believed that the jaguar was a god who helped the sun to travel beneath the world each night, ensuring that it rose again each morning. Incidents of humans being followed through the jungle by lone jaguars are probably attributable to curiosity.

MOUNTAIN LION
(*Puma concolor*)

Known as cougars, pumas, painters, and catamounts, mountain lions are the New World's second-largest felids. Portrayed as dangerous to people in novels and movies, there have been rare instances where pumas have attacked humans. Usually the cat is an old one, with bad teeth, failing health, and perhaps debilitating arthritis that keeps it from catching prey as well as it used to.

Human victims are typically small statured, alone in rural areas, and engaged in an activity that excites the feline hunting instinct the same way a wriggling string triggers a compulsive instinct in house cats to attack. Breathless joggers and running children are likely victims, but skiers, snowshoers, and backpackers virtually never because they appear too large to be easy prey; the objective of any predator is not to fight but to subdue prey with as little danger to itself as possible.

Geographic Range

The mountain lion once had a range that spanned the New World from southern Argentina to northern Canada and from one ocean to the other. Conflict between cats and people peaked as a result of increased housing development along the Pacific coast in the early 1990s. This brought the big cats into conflict with homeowners, and state authorities reinstated a hunting season. Animal rights groups responded by illegally livetrapping and transplanting cougars, and by 1994 the animals were being spotted in Pennsylvania, Wisconsin, and Michigan's Lower Peninsula—places where the species had long been extinct.

Habitat

Mountain lions can utilize a broad range of habitats, from subtropical jungle and northern cedar swamps to alpine forest and desert mountains. Deep snows, craggy rock, and thick undergrowth are not limiting factors. Essentially, the cougars are capable of existing anyplace where they can find water, concealing cover, and enough deer-size prey to keep them well fed.

Physical Characteristics

Mass: Mountain lions weigh 75 to 275 pounds.

Body: The body is muscular and lithe, like a domestic cat. Body length is 60 to 108 inches; legs are short and thick, with powerful hindquarters that create a jacked-up appearance. Skull is broad and short, with a high arched forehead and a broad rostrum (nasal bone). Nose pad is large and triangle-shaped; ears are short and rounded. The mandible is powerfully constructed, carnassial (scissoring) teeth are massive, and long canines enable quick kills on large prey. The upper jaw holds one more premolar on each side than either the bobcat or lynx. Molars have a scissorlike fit, designed not for crushing bone (like scavengers) but for cutting hide and flesh.

Tail: The tail is one-third of total length, 21 to 36 inches long, and tawny brown with a black tip.

Tracks: Prints are more round than the elongated tracks of canids. Front prints are 3 to more than 4 inches long; hind tracks are about 10 percent smaller. Four large toes show in all tracks (front dewclaw doesn't register) but normally with no claws showing because of retractable claws. Heel pads of front and hind feet have three lobes, but the front pads are more blocky, less rounded. Walking stride is 20 inches, straddle is 8 inches.

Scat: Scat is similar to that of canids; segmented, cylindrical, tapered at one or both ends; about 5 inches long by 1 to 1.5 inches in diameter. Deer hair wraps around the outer surface in spiral fashion to prevent sharp bones encased within from scratching the intestines.

Coloration: The pelage is short and fairly coarse. Upper body ranges from tan to reddish brown in summer, becoming darker and grayer during winter. The chest, underbelly, and mouth area of the muzzle are white, becoming more yellowed with age. The backs of the ears are black. A dark stripe extends downward around the muzzle at either side of the pinkish nose. The eyes of adults range from bright yellow to gray-yellow.

Sign: Claw marks in trees serve as territorial scratching posts, but the span and thickness of claw marks are much broader than those of a bobcat or lynx. Scats haphazardly covered with soil show claw marks that are usually from the same direction in which the cat was traveling.

Vocalizations: Mountain lions purr when content or when mothers are suckling kittens and can mew like house cats. Other vocalizations include hisses, growls, and the trademark snarl. Kittens mew like domestic kittens but have a loud chirping cry that gets their mother's attention.

Life span: Couagrs live about ten years in the wild, up to twenty years in captivity.

Diet

Like all felids, cougars prefer to hunt rather than to eat carrion. Superbly equipped with stealth, speed, and natural armament, a puma can take down prey larger than itself, typically leaping onto the backs of large animals and dispatching them with a brain-piercing bite to the base of the skull.

Most famed for taking deer-size game, a mountain lion also eats most smaller-size animals and can survive well on a diet that includes no large prey. When the quarry is large, a puma prefers to concentrate on immature or sickly individuals that won't put up a hard fight. Annual food consumption for an adult cat is 600 to 900 pounds.

Mating Habits

Cougars are normally solitary, but when they join to mate, it's a polygamous relationship, with both genders typically breeding with more than one partner. Both sexes mature at two and a half years, but males won't mate until they have established their own territories, usually at three years. Males remain sexually fertile for up to twenty years, females to about twelve years. Copulation is preceded by several days of courtship that allow a pair to become accustomed to one another. There is no fixed mating season, but breeding generally occurs from December to March. Males respond to pheromonal scents, yowling, and other vocalizations from females with their own eerie caterwauling, sounding much like large alley cats.

Female mountain lions mate every other year, with the mother devoting off years to teaching offspring the skills of survival. The estrus period lasts nine days, but if the female hasn't achieved pregnancy before a heat passes, she will come into estrus for another nine-day cycle.

Mating battles between males are mostly bloodless, consisting largely of body language. When males do fight, contests are largely of physical strength, without claws or teeth. Injuries do occur, but mountain lions harbor an instinctive revulsion against harming their own kind, and their decidedly lethal weapons are not used with the violence that they could be.

Gestation lasts eighty-two to ninety-six days, with mothers giving birth in a secluded cave or den within the father's territory. Litter sizes range from one to six cubs, with three or four being average. Newborns weigh between one and two pounds and are blind and helpless for their first ten days of life. The cubs' first teeth erupt immediately thereafter, and they begin to play. The father may bring the female food during the denning period, but he takes no role in rearing offspring. At forty days the cubs are weaned and accompany their mother on short hunting forays.

Male cubs remain with the mother for one year before leaving to establish their own territories; female cubs may remain with her for up to two years. Emancipated cubs may remain together for a short time, using the strength of numbers to discourage would-be predators.

Behaviorisms

A mountain lion's solitary lifestyle is interrupted only by breeding and rearing of young. Territorial ranges vary downward from about 60 square miles, depending on the availability of food and water. Residents of either sex mark their territories with urine or fecal deposits, often at the bases of trees that serve as scratching posts.

Cougars are primarily nocturnal, with excellent night and binocular vision. Their main sense is sight, followed by sense of smell, then hearing. Pumas typically have summer and winter ranges in different locations because they follow the migratory habits of deer.

Mountain lions are hunted as sport, and their pelts have considerable trophy value as rugs or wall hangings. They can be a threat to domestic animals but tend to avoid human habitation.

BOBCAT
(*Lynx rufus*)

The bobcat is America's most widespread and successful wild cat.

The bobcat is the most dominant wild felid in North America, and this highly adaptable species is comfortable in a broad range of habitats. Having been hunted, trapped, or poisoned to near extinction in some places, bobcats are shy of humans and are rarely seen. That secretiveness may lessen as housing development continues to bring humans into bobcat habitats.

Geographic Range

Bobcats are found throughout North America from southern Mexico to southern Canada and from the Atlantic to the Pacific coasts. Population densities in the United States are higher in the forested eastern region than they are in western states. The species is rare or nonexistent in the large agricultural regions of southern Michigan, Illinois, Indiana, Ohio, and Pennsylvania.

Habitat

Bobcats can adapt to a wide variety of habitats, including dense forests, wet swamps, semi-arid deserts, forested mountains, and brushland. They prefer plenty of cover with trees large enough to climb for the purpose of observation or escape. The species seems well adapted to cold and snow but isn't found in most of Canada.

Physical Characteristics

Mass: Bobcats weigh 14 to more than 68 pounds and are largest in the north.

Body: The body is much like a domestic cat; lithe, well muscled, and built for agility. Cheeks and ear tips are tufted, though not to the extent of the lynx. Body length is 28 to 50 inches; shoulder height is 15 to 20 inches.

Tail: The tail is short, black-tipped, and 3 to 6 inches long—longer than that of the lynx.

Tracks: The tracks are 1 to 2 inches long, some as long as 3.5 inches in the far north. Four toes are on each foot, with no claws showing. All four feet are approximately the same size. Stride is 10 to 14 inches, straddle is 6 to 7 inches. Hind prints may register precisely inside front tracks, leaving an apparently bipedal track pattern. Front of heel pad, toward toes, is concave and distinctly different from any of the canids.

Scat: Scat is cylindrical, segmented, tapered at one or both ends. Length is 2 to 6 inches, diameter is 0.5 to 1 inch, with rodent, rabbit, or deer fur wound in a spiral fashion around small bones encased within. Scats are indistinguishable from those of the lynx and easily confused with those of a coyote or fox, except that canids don't attempt to cover scats with dirt.

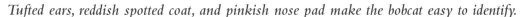

Tufted ears, reddish spotted coat, and pinkish nose pad make the bobcat easy to identify.

Unlike cougars, which tend to scratch earth from the direction in which they'll be traveling, bobcats scratch from all directions, leaving raylike patterns of scratch marks all around the scat deposit.

Coloration: The bobcat's summer pelage is darker brown spots against a coat of brown or reddish brown; the winter coat tends to be darker, with spots less obvious, ranging from dark brown to almost gray. In all seasons the insides of the legs, underbelly, and throat are cream colored to white (darkest in older individuals), mottled with brown spots.

Sign: Deep scratches in smooth-barked tree trunks, about two feet above the ground, are often scented with the cat's pungent urine. Soft pines seem to be the preferred scratching posts, possibly because the strong-smelling sap helps to conceal the bobcat's own scent.

Vocalizations: The bobcat sounds much like a domestic cat, with noises consisting of soft mews, purring, low growls, and childlike wailing during the breeding season.

Life span: Bobcats live eight to ten years in the wild.

Diet

A bobcat's diet includes prey that ranges from small mice to rabbits to an occasional fawn. The species rarely eats carrion, preferring to kill its own food. Like house cats, bobcats have an uncanny ability to sneak within striking distance of prey. Blue jays, grouse, and other birds are caught before they can fly away from this wildcat's lightning-fast attack. Yearling deer may be taken in deep winter snows, usually by strong cats perched on an overhead tree branch. When a likely victim comes into range, the cat pounces onto its back, anchors itself with hooklike retractable claws, and drives long, sharp canines into the base of the victim's skull. When forced to take prey head-on, the cat may instead clamp its mouth over the windpipe, suffocating the victim.

Officially a carnivore, the bobcat's diet of meat is supplemented with berries and vegetation. Sugar calories from blueberries and other fruits help to put on fat against the approaching winter and provide nutrients that are lacking in meat. Indigestible grasses and sedges are also eaten to help scour intestines and colon.

Mating Habits

Bobcats in the northern range mate in February or March, but those in the South may breed throughout summer; in especially warm areas, females may produce two litters a year. Mating is initiated by the scent of a female coming into heat, which may attract numerous suitors. After a contest that consists mostly of caterwauling,

This fresh bobcat scat, about a half-inch in diameter, contains small rodent bones, wrapped in a protective outer sheath of fur.

growls, and an occasional scuffle, the strongest male mates with the receptive female, and the pair sets off to find a sheltered birthing den in a rock crevice or hollow log or under the roots of a large standing tree. Poor diggers, bobcats may appropriate existing fox or coyote dens.

After a gestation period of sixty to seventy days, the mother gives birth to a litter of two or three blind kittens, each weighing eight ounces, in late April or May. After ten days the young open their eyes and move about the den. The mother stays with the kittens constantly for their first two months, leaving only to drink and to relieve herself. During this time her mate, who doesn't enter the den, brings food and guards the den when she's away.

Kittens are weaned in June or July, and the parents separate, the male taking no role in rearing the offspring. Kittens hunt with their mother, learning the finer points of catching meals and avoiding danger, until they reach eight months, usually in December or January. Nearly grown then, males leave first, followed within a month by their sisters. Young adults disperse widely but generally travel no farther than is necessary. Emancipated kittens will likely take—or at least compete for—a mate in their first breeding season.

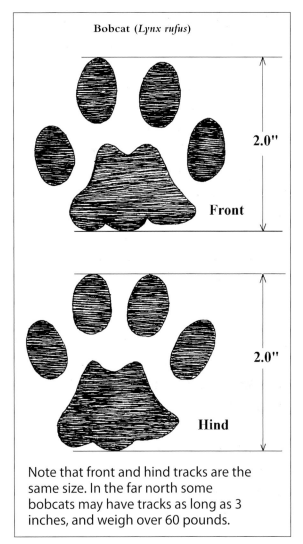

Bobcat (*Lynx rufus*)

2.0"

Front

2.0"

Hind

Note that front and hind tracks are the same size. In the far north some bobcats may have tracks as long as 3 inches, and weigh over 60 pounds.

Behaviorisms

The solitary bobcat interacts only to mate. Females live discreetly, especially if they have kittens, but males blatantly advertise their claim to a territory of about five square miles. Partly buried scats left at trail intersections delineate territory. Odorous sprays of urine on tree trunks that may be marked by clawing do the same.

The home range of a dominant male bobcat typically overlaps the domains of several females, giving the resident male a head start at detecting when one of them comes into estrus. The territorial boundaries of two males may overlap, but this seldom leads to conflict except during mating season or if food becomes scarce.

Bobcats don't normally live in dens, but there may be several refuges sited throughout an individual's range. The dens serve as shelter for escaping foul weather that also drives most prey into hiding or for eluding larger predators.

LYNX
(*Lynx canadensis*)

The most northern and most secretive of American wild cats, the lynx is a symbol of wilderness.

This slightly smaller but lankier cousin to the bobcat is one of the most reclusive species in North America. Lynx are supremely adapted to life in the dense timber and deep snows of the far north woods. Lynx pelts—mostly from Canada—have become increasingly valuable since restrictions were placed on the importation of cat pelts in the latter half of the 20th century. Lynx populations have never been in danger.

Geographic Range

The largest populations of lynx are found throughout Canada and in the northernmost regions of Montana and Idaho. There are small populations in New England, northern Wisconsin, and Michigan's Upper Peninsula. With a demonstrated aversion to humans, warming winters, and a continually shrinking habitat, lynx are unlikely to ever be common.

Habitat

Native to North America, lynx are occasionally seen on tundra or in rocky areas in the far north but never far from dense old-growth forests and thick swamps that are its required habitat. Lynx are superbly adapted to life in deep snow but have a pronounced tendency to avoid humans, so anyone who sees one in the wild can count that day lucky.

Physical Characteristics

Mass: Lynx weigh 11 to 40 pounds.

Body: Lynx are long legged with very large, furry paws adapted for silent travel atop deep snow. Body length is 29 to 41 inches, and males are about 10 percent larger than females. Pointed ears are tipped with long tufts of fur; cheeks are also tufted, giving the appearance of sideburns. Shoulder height is 15 to more than 20 inches.

Tail: The tail is shorter than the bobcat's, 2 to 5 inches long.

Tracks: Four toes are on each foot, with no claws showing in tracks. Paws are extraordinarily large and well furred, especially in winter, making tracks appear even larger and giving this fast runner an edge when pursuing prey over deep snow. Fore print is 3 to 4.5 inches long, hind prints are about 10 percent smaller. Hind print has three lobes at rear of heel pad, and front print has three lobes on heel pad, but the two outermost lobes extend more to the rear at either side, leaving a chevron-shaped impression unlike the three equal-sized lobes made by the front heel pad of a bobcat. Stride is 14 to 16 inches, straddle is 5 to 7 inches.

Scat: Scat is usually indistinguishable from bobcat scats, being cylindrical, segmented, and tapered at one or both ends. Length is 2 to 6 inches, diameter is 0.5 to 1 inch. Scats are usually only partially buried under soil or snow and typically have an outer covering of fine hare or rabbit fur wrapped spirally around an inner core of small bones.

Coloration: There is some variation, but the usual lynx coat is yellow-brown in summer, becoming grayer in winter, and longer than the fur of a bobcat. Individuals may have dark

Lynx scat, about 1-inch in diameter, encased in a sheath of fine squirrel and hare fur.

spots, but lynx generally lack the heavily spotted appearance of a bobcat. The ear tufts and tip of the tail are black, and the throat, belly, and insides of the legs are whitish. Yellow eyes denote good night vision.

Sign: Sign includes scent posts on smooth-barked trees that have been clawed and sprayed with urine and partially covered scats left at trail intersections. Large prey that cannot be eaten immediately will often be cached by burying it beneath debris or snow.

Vocalizations: Lynx are normally silent except during the mating season, when males especially utter a loud shriek or scream that ends with an echoing wail some people have described as eerie, like the wailing of a small child.

Life span: Lynx live eight to ten years in the wild.

Diet

A key species in the lynx diet is the snowshoe, or varying, hare (*Lepus americanus*). Being at least as proficient a hunter as its cousin, the bobcat, the lynx is capable of catching rodents, birds, spawning fish, and an occasional yearling deer, but survival of this species relies heavily on snowshoe hare populations. When hare populations rise and then fall in cycles, as they do about every nine and a half years, lynx populations suffer starvation and starvation-related diseases one year later. Lynx may eat carrion if the meat is fresh and not decayed.

Mating Habits

Like northern bobcats (and unlike southern bobcats), female lynx come into heat only once a year, in March and April, and raise only one litter per year. Prior to selecting her mate, a receptive female may have several suitors follow her everywhere with wailing, caterwauling,

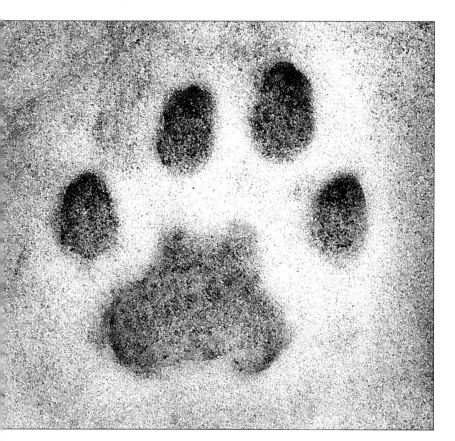

and an occasional fight marked by lots of hissing, spitting, and growling but little bloodshed. After about one week of this competition, the female enters an estrus period of one to two days and selects a mate. After mating, the pair leaves to find a secluded birthing den in a hollow log or rock crevice.

After a gestation period of nine weeks, females give birth in May or June to two (and sometimes as many as five) blind kittens, each weighing about seven ounces.

Right front track of a lynx; note that the broad foot—nature's own snowshoe—presses evenly into the snow all around, denoting excellent balance and stealth.

Larger litter sizes are indicative of an especially healthy mother and abundant food. Except for short departures to drink or relieve herself, the mother remains with her young constantly for their first month of life, relying on her mate to bring food and keep watch against enemies. After one month the kittens begin eating meat, but continue to nurse for five months, and are weaned in October or November.

After weaning, when the kittens have grown enough to travel, the male lynx leaves and takes no part in rearing his offspring. The nearly grown young remain with their mother until January or February before setting off on their own, with males usually leaving first. Freed of her charges, the mother will come into heat again about one month later. Her female kittens reach sexual maturity at twenty-one months, males at thirty-three months.

Behaviorisms

Lynx are solitary animals, generally avoiding one another except to mate. They are territorial, but a male's domain is likely to infringe upon the territories of several females. Territories vary from 7 to more than 200 square miles, depending on the availability of food and resources.

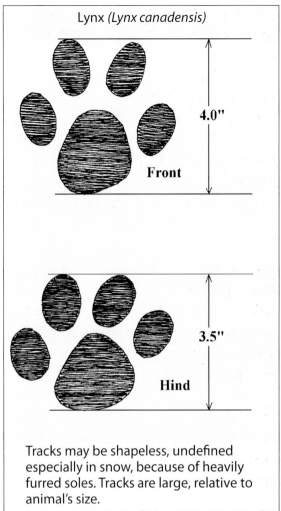

Lynx *(Lynx canadensis)*

4.0"

Front

3.5"

Hind

Tracks may be shapeless, undefined especially in snow, because of heavily furred soles. Tracks are large, relative to animal's size.

Lynx are primarily nocturnal, with excellent night vision and keen directional hearing. They lie in wait for hours along game trails, overlooking them from a tree branch or knoll, or they might stalk a prey to within a few yards, then pounce onto its back. Long canine teeth deliver a fatal bite to the base of the victim's skull, enabling these cats to swiftly take down animals large enough to be dangerous to them. Hard times prompt females with young to hunt cooperatively for hares, spreading themselves into a skirmish line and moving through brushy areas until one of them jumps prey. This hunting technique appears to be learned rather than instinctual.

Lynx shelter from foul weather in rough dens under rock ledges, in caves, under fallen trees, or in hollow logs. There are likely to be several such refuges scattered throughout an animal's territory.

Family Ursidae

Bears live in North America, northern Europe, Asia, and India. All are large and powerfully built, ranging from up to 600 pounds for a mature black bear to more than 1,700 pounds for the massive Kodiak brown bear. All have five toes on each foot, each toe tipped with a stout, functional claw.

Until the late 20th century, it was believed that bears hibernated, but today we know that bears don't enter the comalike torpor of true hibernators and sometimes leave their dens to wander during midwinter warm spells.

Most interesting to scientists are the bears' physiological attributes. Despite putting on about 25 percent of body weight in fat each year, bears suffer no arterial blockage from cholesterol. Denned bears neither defecate nor urinate for months at a time; they have a remarkable renal system that not only isn't poisoned from a buildup of nitrogen urea but also converts that lethal waste product into usable amino acids, then recycles the water for use in bodily functions. If scientists can learn how a bear reprocesses its own urine, the positive implications for humans suffering from kidney failure could be enormous. NASA, too, is keenly interested in how a bear can remain inactive for several months without experiencing the loss of bone mass suffered by human astronauts.

BLACK BEAR
(*Ursus americanus*)

Smallest of North America's three native bear species, the black bear is the most abundant, adaptable, and widespread. Black bears avoid contact with humans, and people in the midst of black bear country seldom see one. Smokey Bear, fire prevention icon of the U.S. Forest Service, is a black bear.

Geographic Range

Native only to North America, black bears were once common throughout the continent, but today their range is half what it was. The species is found south of the Arctic Circle throughout Canada and Alaska from the Pacific to the Atlantic, from northern California to the Rocky Mountains, southward along the Rockies to central Mexico, and along the eastern seaboard from Maine down to Florida.

Ursus americanus is unique to North America, reaching weights in excess of 600 pounds and able to thrive in most environments.

Habitat

Black bear habitat is forested, with large trees that can be climbed to escape danger. In the course of a single year, a bear might travel as far as 500 miles, following plants, fish, and other foods as they become available.

Physical Characteristics

Mass: Black bears weigh 200 to more than 600 pounds, and males are about 5 percent larger than females.

Body: They are powerfully muscled, covered by thick fur, and especially large in autumn, when animals carry 25 percent of total weight in body fat. Body length is 4 to 6 feet. Head is round, with a short muzzle and erect rounded ears.

Tail: The tail is short, furred, and 3 to 7 inches long.

Tracks: There are five forward-pointing toes on each foot, each tipped with a curved and sharply pointed claw that enables black bears to scale trees. Front tracks are 4 to 5 inches long, 6 to 7 inches if heel pad registers (usually as a large dot). Hind prints are 7 to 9 inches, long, 5 inches wide at the toes, resembling a human footprint. The largest toe is outermost, opposite our own. The normal walk is a shuffling gait, with a stride of about 1 foot, a straddle of 10 to 12 inches.

The running gait is the quadrupedal "rocking-horse" pattern: forefeet are planted together as the hind feet come forward on either side; when the hind feet hit the ground, the forelegs and back are extended as the animal leaps forward, coming down again on paired forefeet, and the gait repeats.

Scat: Scat is cylindrical, dark brown to black, with flat, untapered ends; insect legs or carapaces may be apparent. When the animal is feeding on meat, scats become carnivore-like, tapered at one or both ends, with small bones and fragments sheathed within a spiral of fur. Length is 2 to 8 inches; diameter is 1 to 2 inches. Rich diets cause cow-pie-like scats.

Coloration: Black bears are usually coal black, brown patches covering either side of the muzzle, bordering a black stripe that extends from top of the muzzle to nose pad. Young bears up to two years may have a spot of white on the chest. Black bears west of the Great Lakes are frequently brown and misidentified as brown bears, but they lack the distinctive shoulder hump. A bluish phase occurs near Alaska's Yakutat Peninsula, and those on Gribble Island are almost completely white; all three color phases are found in British Columbia.

Sign: Scat deposits at trail intersections mark territorial boundaries. Trees are used as scratching posts, with five usually deep gouges extending vertically down the trunk from a height of up to 7 feet or as high as the maker could reach. Scratches are a visual record of a bear's size, but interdigital scents (akin to sweat from human palms) carries information about gender, size, and individual identification. Green trees are sometimes scratched, but standing dead trees seem to be preferred, as well as bridges, fence posts, and power poles. Sows, especially those with cubs, are less obvious, so most of the territorial sign a tracker finds will have been left there by males.

Other sign includes excavations that were dug in pursuit of rodents, rotting logs that have been ripped apart, and fruit trees clawed or split apart at their crotches to reach upper branches.

Vocalizations: Black bears are normally silent. A chomping of teeth accompanied by a froth of saliva at the corners of the mouth indicates anxiety. A loud huffing is another warning to leave, and low bawling sounds are used by mothers to communicate with offspring. Bears bawl loudly during territorial wrestling matches.

Life span: Black bears live up to thirty years in captivity; life span in the wild is about fifteen years.

Rich, nutritious blueberries are a much sought-after food source by many species from late summer through autumn, as this purple bear scat shows.

A typical solid bear scat, seen when an animal's diet is omnivorous, consisting of rodent hairs, plant fibers, and insect exoskeletons. Note that ends are nearly squared, not tapered, like most carnivore scats.

Diet

Black bears are omnivorous, and their digestive system can assimilate the rough grass fibers with nearly the same efficiency as a deer. Fat-rich larvae are favored, along with spiders, frogs, and fish. Bears sometimes knock off the tops of anthills and then insert a forefoot into the mass of angered insects; when the paw is covered by attacking ants, the bear licks them off. A black bear's diet varies widely from one season or region to another.

With a running speed of about 30 miles per hour, black bears cannot run down large prey. They appropriate kills from more-skilled hunters if an opportunity presents itself, and they are well equipped for excavating burrowed squirrels. One exception is in late spring, when black bears prowl the thickets in search of newborn fawns.

A black bear's territory may encompass several hundred square miles but seldom more than is necessary to obtain enough nutrition to put on a quarter of its body weight in fat for the coming winter.

One phenomenon that trackers should be alert for in spring is the anal plug of mostly grasses that blocks the colon during the winter sleep. Prior to denning, bears eat a last meal of rough, indigestible sedges and grasses, which mass together in the lower intestine. The plug ensures that no excrement fouls the den during sleep—especially not birthing dens. Expelled anal plugs are cylindrical, two to three inches long, and composed of grass blades, plant fibers, and pine needles, coated with a mucouslike fluid when fresh. Bears remain close to their dens for about a week after waking, so a freshly expelled anal plug indicates that a bear den is nearby.

Black bears leave the feet of squirrel-size and larger prey, biting them free of the carcass as it feeds. The purpose is to remove the sharp climbing claws that could injure the bear's convoluted digestive system, which is unlike the straighter intestines of true carnivores.

Crushed Reindeer Moss lichens show the left hind and left front tracks of a bear walking toward the right of this photo. Forefoot is behind rear foot; note identifying dot shape pressed into the lichens at far left.

Mating Habits

Males older than three years pair with females older than two years in June and July for two weeks of courtship. After mating, they separate, with males to mate again, if possible. At this time females with two-year-old cubs abandon them to mate again.

Bears den in November and December, and only then do fertilized eggs (carried dormant by the sow within her womb) implant to the uterine wall and begin to develop. If a sow is sickly or malnourished, the eggs involuntarily abort. If a pregnant female is healthy and strong, litter size may increase from twins to as many as five cubs.

Black bear dens are inconspicuous and remote, ranging from dugouts under the roots of a large tree to dry culverts under remote two-tracks. Den entrances are just large enough for occupants to squeeze through into a larger sleeping chamber. A small space loses less warmth than a more voluminous area, so den sizes are small and efficient.

Cubs are born in January and February, after a gestation of ten weeks. Hairless and blind, eight-ounce newborns instinctively make their way to a nipple. Once attached, cubs remain there most of the time until spring, growing rapidly. Because black bears are not true hibernators, the mother's body tempera-

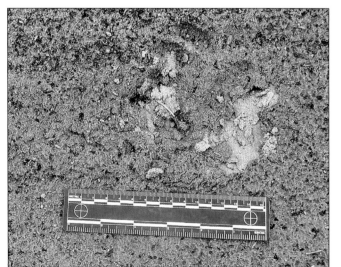

Left front black bear track in rain-dampened sand, identifiable by five forward-pointing toes, and extra-deep impression left by the largest, outermost toe when the animal stepped off.

ture remains almost normal throughout winter, keeping offspring warm while she sleeps.

When mother and newborns leave the den in April or May, youngsters will weigh from two to five pounds. Cubs travel with the mother on her annual migration, learning the foraging and watering places that they may continue to visit throughout their own lives. By eight months the cubs are weaned and weigh 25 pounds or more. They can forage for insects and grasses and catch an occasional rodent or frog, but they are still prey for wolves and larger bears.

By the end of their first summer, cubs weigh about 75 pounds, and the white blaze on their chests has faded to black. The cubs' mother will not mate in their first year, devoting all her time and energy to teaching and protecting her young. When she dens at the onset of winter, the cubs, who have also acquired a thick layer of fat, will den with her. When mother and cubs awaken in spring, she continues their educations until June, when the youngsters, now eighteen months old and weighing about 100 pounds, are abandoned or chased off so that the mother may mate again. Female cubs may breed at two years, but males probably not until they've established their own territories, usually at three or four years. Females breed every other year until about age nine; males are sexually active until about twelve years.

Behaviorisms

Black bears are most active at dawn and dusk (crepuscular), although breeding and feeding activities may alter their patterns. Except for mating season, the overriding purpose in a bear's life is to feed continuously from spring until denning in early winter. This behavior is an evolved response to sleeping through winter, when normal foods are unavailable. A bear foraging in deep snows would have little chance of survival, but sleeping through winter requires taking enough nutrition into the den with them to survive for four or five months without eating.

The right forefoot of this bear cub shows the sharp hooked claws that enable black bears to climb trees and catch fish better than straighter-clawed brown bears. Note distinctive round pad at rear, which prints as a large dot to the rear of foreprints (also seen with brown bears).

The right hind foot of this yearling black bear shows the humanlike configuration of an animal that walks plantigrade fashion, or flat-footed.

The solitary nature of black bears depends on food availability; well equipped to catch fish with their sharply hooked claws, black bears sometimes come together along stream banks where suckers, trout, and salmon spawn. Similar congregations may be found in large tracts of ripening berries and at landfills.

During the 20th century it was a favorite pastime for motorists to visit municipal dumps at dusk to watch black bears rummage through human garbage. Dump bears get along well, so long as they respect one another's space, but human observers got into trouble, so today most garbage dumps are gated and locked after business hours.

Black bears are known to take easily killed livestock, but predations are rare. More real is the damage they can inflict on corn crops, apple and cherry orchards, and bee yards. With their need to feed bolstered by intelligence, curiosity, and immense physical strength, black bears do

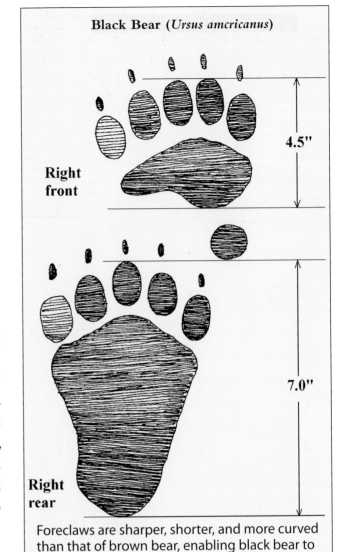

Black Bear (*Ursus amcricanus*)

Right front

4.5"

Right rear

7.0"

Foreclaws are sharper, shorter, and more curved than that of brown bear, enabling black bear to climb trees.

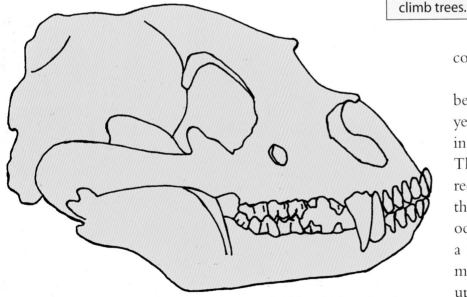

The black bear's jaw is a model of multi-functional design, with canine weapons, camassial cutters, and grinding molars that enable it to eat almost any food.

considerable damage to crops.

Approximately 30,000 black bears are killed by hunters each year, nationwide, but the species is in no danger from overharvesting. There have been numerous cases of recently emancipated cubs wandering the streets of rural towns, attracted by odors emanating from dumpsters. In a few instances the trespassing animals have been shot dead, but public uproar has caused local authorities to adopt less lethal means of removal.

Black bears normally pose no danger to people; thirty-six humans

Despite being equipped with natural weapons that can kill, these bears, like all wild species, fight only until it becomes evident which of them is stronger.

were killed by black bears in all of the 20th century—fewer than are killed each year by dogs. Mothers with small cubs are most likely to send them up a tree, climbing up after them and waiting for the danger to pass. Few hikers in black bear country will ever see one.

Rarely, bears in the summer rut have stood their ground or even approached a human. The most unbending rule in an encounter is to never run; no human can outrun a bear, and running away excites the animal's predatory instincts, causing it to give chase. Standing fast in the face of a bear charge that nearly always turns out to be a bluff isn't easy, but a person who appears strong is less likely to be mauled.

In rare instances where *Ursus americanus* can legitimately be accused of attacking a person, the intent has been predatory. Few animals eat human flesh, but an old or sickly bear that faces starvation because it can no longer make the long seasonal trek to follow its food supply might be tempted to prey on a human.

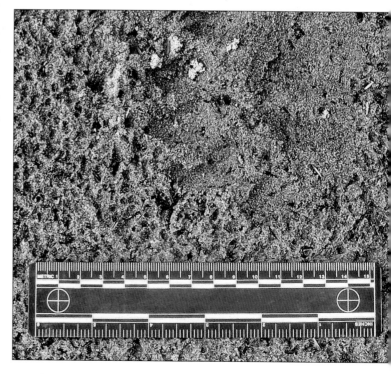

The right hind track of a bear in rain-soaked sand. Heel of the humanlike foot did not print because bears and most other species walk with weight forward, on the toes.

BROWN BEAR
(*Ursus arctos horribilis*—the suffix *horribilis* is sometimes dropped)

The massive and powerful brown bear, President Teddy Roosevelt's personal icon, resides at the top of the food chain throughout the north.

By weight, the brown bear is the largest land carnivore in the world, reaching twice the size of a black bear, and is heavier than the taller polar bear. On the basis of the accounts of field researchers such as Doug Peacock, author of *Grizzly Years*, and anglers who fish with brown bears at Alaska's Denali National Park, the species is neither afraid of nor hungry for humans. Like the normally harmless black bear, there have been instances where an old or sickly individual preyed on a human because it was starving, but in general, brown bears do not regard *Homo sapiens* as edible.

Geographic Range

Brown bears once roamed across the northern hemisphere from the Arctic Circle to Central America. An estimated population of 100,000 can still be found in northern Eurasia, with about 70,000 of those living in Russia. Isolated sightings have been reported from the Atlas Mountains of northernmost Africa and possibly on Japan's Hokkaido Island. In the 20th cen-

The right front paw of this brown bear dug deeply into the damp sand when the animal changed direction, while its broader hind foot left a much lighter impression.

tury, brown bear populations in the lower forty-eight fell from more than 100,000 animals at the turn of the century to a current low of about 1,000. Brown bear populations in Alaska and western Canada remain stable at an estimated 30,000 individuals.

Habitat

Brown bears are at home in most habitats, but the species seems partial to semi-open areas like alpine meadows and brushy tundra. Brown bears were a common sight on the Great Plains when the first European immigrants arrived. With a digestive system that can assimilate plants nearly as well as deer, the bears are at home on the plains, but never far from a thicket in which to sleep. In Siberia, brown bears are creatures of the deep forest, while European populations prefer mountain woodlands. So long as a habitat provides food, water, and a secluded place to rest, *Ursus arctos* can live there.

Physical Characteristics

Mass: Brown bears weigh 400 to more than 1,700 pounds, and males are 10 percent larger than females.

Body: They are powerfully built, with a distinctive large hump of muscle between the shoulders. Shoulder height is 4 to 4.5 feet; body length is 6 to more than 7 feet; standing height is 10 feet or more. The head is large and broad, with small, round ears. Facial profile is

Brown and black bear scats are often identical in composition when both are feeding in the same areas, and scats of both species can be quite varied, depending on diet. This large, cowpie-like scat reflects a rich diet of mostly berries and wild cherries.

almost concave, giving the impression of an upturned nose, unlike the rounded muzzle and profile of a black bear.

Tail: The tail is about 3 inches long and well furred.

Tracks: Tracks are similar to those of the black bear but larger; five toes are on all four feet, with almost straight claws extending from the front toes to a length of 3 inches or more. Forefeet are 5 to 6 inches long, discounting the dot-shaped heel-pad impression that may print 3 or 4 inches to the rear of the forefoot heel pad; forefoot width is 8 to 10 inches. Hind feet are 10 to 16 inches long, 7 to 8 inches wide, elongated, almost human shaped, and tipped with shorter claws.

Scat: Scat is similar to a black bear's but usually larger; cylindrical, segmented, and dark brown to black when fresh, with evidence of seeds, grasses, and berries. Diameter may exceed 2 inches. A single scat may be broken into several segments of 2 to 4 inches in length, or, if the animal is feeding on rich meats, it might be coiled and in a single piece. Rodent and deer hair may be wrapped spiral fashion around the outside.

Coloration: Fur is usually dark brown but varies from blond to nearly black in some individuals. The term "grizzly bear" stems from the white-frosted (or grizzled) appearance of the bear's shoulders and back. The brown bear's muzzle is the same color or darker than its pelage but never lighter colored like the black bear's.

Sign: Sign includes excavations in hillsides and meadows where ground squirrel burrows have been dug out, large rocks and downed logs overturned, bathtub-size depressions in the humus of brushy thickets where a bear slept, and clawed logs and standing trees clawed to a height of 9 feet or more.

Vocalizations: Sounds include grunts, growls, huffing, and bawling. Clacking of teeth, often accompanied by a froth of saliva around the mouth, indicates anxiety, and trackers who witness such behavior should withdraw immediately but slowly, never turning their backs to the bear.

Life span: Brown bears live up to forty-seven years in captivity but normally less than thirty-five years in the wild. Potential life span has been estimated to be up to fifty years.

Diet

Brown bears have an efficient digestive system; in spring, before many food plants have sprouted, sedges, roots, and lichens constitute the bulk of a bear's diet. As the warm season progresses and more plants mature, a bear's diet and travels change to match available foods. Calorie-rich berries, pine nuts, and fruits are preferred, and several types of fungi are eaten.

Insects are on the menu, too. Rotting logs and stumps provide larvae whose bodies are composed mostly of fat. Bears eat spiders as they hang in their webs, and ants are gathered when the bear sticks a paw into their hill, licking the attacking insects off with its raspy tongue.

Brown bears will eat carrion they find or can appropriate from other carnivores. The seemingly instinctive hatred between wolves and bears probably stems from the brown bear's

A bear den excavated into the side of a hill, sometimes under the roots of a large tree, will always have an entrance just large enough for its owner to squeeze through, opening into a large chamber within. (Photo courtesy USFWS.)

Brown bear tracks along a sandy shoreline show this bear's fearless and unhurried disposition.

practice of stealing carcasses brought down by hunting packs. Brown bears also prey on wolf pups if they can, but even a pair of wolves is usually sufficient to deter a large brown bear.

In the far north, big Alaskan brown bears frequent fur seal and walrus colonies during their summer mating seasons, seeking out calves, males wounded in mating battles, and individuals weak from age. A brown's 35-mile per hour run is too slow to threaten healthy deer, but bears may follow caribou herds during annual migrations, waiting for weak individuals to fall behind the herd.

Right after the bears emerge from winter dens, but before the summer growing season is under way, most of the meat eaten by a brown bear consists of rodents and ground squirrels dug out of burrows by its massive forepaws. With mice and voles numbering in the thousands per acre, rodents can make up most of a bear's diet in spring. Like badgers, brown bears may be shadowed by a coyote that is there to exploit the bear's work by guarding the prey's escape holes.

Watching grizzlies fish for spawning salmon in spring or fall has become a tourist attraction in places such as Alaska's Denali National Park. Brown bears of all ages, most of whom learned to fish there from their mothers, wait to ambush fish at narrows, rapids, and shallows. Fatty fish flesh is critical to the bears' diet, and they've learned to tolerate one another so that all can share this abundance of rich food. Sows with cubs keep their distance from adult boars, which sometimes kill yearling cubs to force mothers into early estrus.

Mating Habits

Between May and July, sexually mature sows three years or older begin advertising through pheromonal scents. Bears five or six years of age advertise their availability through scat and urine deposits on trails that overlap a female's territory. After a week of courtship, the pair copulate frequently for about three days or until the sow knows she is pregnant. Females probably take only one mate per season.

Sows carry fertilized eggs alive but dormant within their wombs until October or November, when the eggs implant to the uterine wall if the female is healthy and fat, or they spontaneously abort to conserve bodily resources for her own needs. In late January to early March, twins (or as many as four cubs) are born. Because brown bears are not true hibernators, the mother bear's body temperatures remain near normal and bears awaken easily, but birthing mothers may sleep through delivery. Only one pound at birth, blind and naked cubs make their way to a nipple and nestle into their mother's belly fur to nurse continuously until she awakens in April or May. At that point the cubs are fully furred and able to travel with their mother as she begins the same annual foraging trek to seasonal food sources that they will make as adults and teach to their own offspring.

At five months, in late June to early August, cubs are weaned and begin to forage for themselves on grasses, forbs, and insects. Mothers share kills with the cubs, but they soon learn to catch rodents, frogs, and other small animals. At the end of their first summer, cubs weigh 50 pounds or more, and most smaller mammals will have become potential prey. Yearling cubs

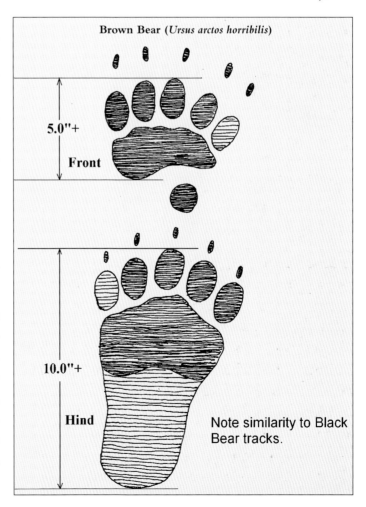

Brown Bear (*Ursus arctos horribilis*)

5.0"+

Front

10.0"+

Hind

Note similarity to Black Bear tracks.

accompany their mothers to rivers to feed on spawning fish but keep their distance from males that might kill them.

Cubs den with their mothers the first winter. When she emerges the following spring, they remain with her until June or July, when she abandons or drives them away so she can mate again. At this time, cubs weigh upward of 150 pounds and aren't easy prey for carnivores. Females are less likely to breed every other year than black bears, and some sows go unmated for up to four years. Young grizzlies establish their own territories, sometimes traveling more than 100 miles to find suitable unclaimed habitat, and continue to grow until ten years of age. Male brown bears in Yellowstone National Park have been sexually active until twenty-five years of age.

Behaviorisms

Ursus arctos may be active at any time of the day, but the species is generally crepuscular. After feeding during the cool night hours, brown bears generally spend the days sleeping in thickets. Be especially careful when hiking in close environments, and be mindful that a surprised grizzly's instinct is to charge, not retreat like a black bear. Carcasses of large animals should be observed only through binoculars, never closer than 100 yards, and from downwind to give warning of your approach. Brown bears camouflage carcasses too large to be eaten at once with a partial covering of leaves and debris. Unfinished carcasses are defended, and you can bet that the owner is nearby.

Territory of a male brown bear may exceed 1,000 square miles, but the average is about 200 square miles and seldom more than is required to meet the bear's needs. Males' territories average seven times larger than those of females and normally overlap the territories of several potential mates. Individuals might spend several weeks in one place, but when available foods are gone, so are the bears. A grizzly's omnivorous diet ensures that a number of food sources are available every month of its waking period.

Brown bear adults can't normally climb trees because their claws—sharply curved to give them that ability when they were cubs—have grown out straighter and longer to make them useful as digging tools. This reflects the brown bear's penchant for open habitat, as opposed to the forested environment preferred by black bears, whose sharp, curved claws permit them to climb even smooth-sided trees. This does not mean that climbing a tree is a good way to escape a brown bear, however, because there have been cases in which a bear used the branches of a large pine as ladder rungs.

Brown bears have frequently been observed pushing against dead standing trees until they topple. The objective is to stun animals that might be holed up inside. Once down, the trunk can be torn apart in search of grubs, ants, and wild honeybee hives.

Family Procyonidae

Procyonids include the lesser pandas of Asia, the ringtail and coati of the southwestern United States and Mexico, and the familiar raccoon. Despite the diversity of species within this family, all have five toes on each foot, all are excellent climbers, all have an omnivorous diet, and all are tough, ferocious fighters.

RACCOON
(*Procyon lotor*)

Intelligent, resourceful, and equipped with handlike forepaws that can manipulate objects nearly as well as our own, the raccoon is a real survivor, able to live in most environments. (Photo courtesy USFWS.)

Few animals are better recognized than the raccoon, with its bandit-masked face and striped tail. Considered prey by raptors and larger carnivores when young, a raccoon is ferocious when cornered, and only the largest predators are willing to tackle one. This game nature

Raccoons (as well as skunks and badgers) are well-known for digging up turtle nests, like this one, in early June, leaving small craters along shorelines that are littered with the remnants of flexible egg shells.

is a good defense against predators whose objective is to kill food without endangering themselves.

Healthy raccoons are harmless to people unless cornered, but they are also a potential vector for rabies, mostly in March or April, and especially when local populations are high. Raccoons can seriously injure even large dogs and have been known to draw dogs into deep water, where they climb onto the dog's head and drown it. A bearlike drive to gain fat against the coming lean winter makes the raccoon a nuisance to even suburbanites by being attracted to the odors of human food.

Geographic Range

Excepting the most open and arid places, raccoons are found throughout the United States from the Pacific to the Atlantic. To the north, their range extends only a little beyond Canada's southern border. To the south, they range deep into Mexico, overlapping more southern cousins, the coati and ringtail.

Habitat

Raccoons are intelligent and adaptable. Preferred habitat includes trees large enough to provide for observation or escape and will always have a source of freshwater. The animals are superb swimmers, able to outdistance most enemies across lakes or rivers, and they require a water source that provides aquatic foods like crayfish, clams, and frogs.

With a similar diet and digestive system, typical raccoon scats resemble miniature bear scats, with a "Tootsie Roll" shape that is unsegmented and flat on both ends, about one-half-inch in diameter.

Physical Characteristics

Mass: Raccoons weigh 12 to 48 pounds, with individuals reaching 60 pounds in the far north.

Body: Raccoons are stocky, muscular, and thickly furred over a layer of insulating fat. Males are generally larger than females, but the largest individuals reported have been old females. Body length is 23 to more than 38 inches, arched back is 8 to more than 12 inches high. Head is small with a short pointed muzzle tipped by a black nose. Ears are erect, rounded, and large.

Tail: The tail is striped with alternating bands of darker fur, 7 to more than 14 inches long.

Tracks: There are five toes on all four feet, each toe tipped with a long, stout claw. Toes are fingerlike, especially on fore feet, with four pointing forward, and a shorter thumblike toe extending to the inside, making front tracks like human handprints. Toe tips leave bulbous

This soft raccoon scat—whose volume suggests a large raccoon of about 50 pounds—reflects a rich diet of fruits and meat.

impressions behind claws. Forefoot length is 2 to 3 inches. Hind feet are flat-soled and elongated, indicating the plantigrade walk of a slow-running, formidable animal. The hind print resembles a human footprint but with features that include four fingerlike toes pointing forward, each terminating in a bulbous tip and claw, and one shorter thumblike toe well to the rear, pointing inward. Hind foot length is 3 to 4 inches.

Procyon lotor's normal gait is a shuffling walk in which the hind feet often scrape the earth as they travel forward, leaving scuff marks to the rear of the hind tracks. Hind prints generally register separately and beside the front tracks at a relaxed walk, because raccoons are narrower at the shoulder than at the hip. The bushy tail may brush over tracks on dusty soils. Stride is up to 2 feet between paired front and hind prints. Straddle is 3 to 4 inches and up to 6 inches in larger specimens.

At a fast run of 15 miles per hour on flat ground, the raccoon gait changes to the universal quadruped rocking-horse gait described in Part One, in which forefeet are planted side by side to act as pivots while the hind feet are brought forward on either side. When the hind feet make contact with earth, the coon springs forward, forefeet extended, and the gait repeats anew. At a hard run, the distance between sets of four tracks can exceed 3 feet.

Scat: Scat is cylindrical and usually unsegmented, diameter constant throughout its length. Ends are typically flat, as though cut off; scat is 2 to 3 inches long and up to 0.5 inch in diameter.

This track pattern shows that the raccoon was startled into flight, pushing off hardest with its left hind foot.

Coloration: The most obvious characteristics of the raccoon are its black mask around the eyes and a bushy tail with up to ten black rings running circumferentially along its length. The pelage is grizzled, with fur color that varies from gray to reddish.

Sign: Sign includes shells of turtle eggs excavated from buried nests along sandy shorelines and crayfish carapaces and empty clamshells at the water's edge.

Vocalizations: A chirring sound is made when the animal is inquisitive or content. Territorial and mating sounds include a wide variety of screeches, snarls, and growls.

Life span: Raccoons have lived up to sixteen years in captivity, but wild raccoons seldom live beyond four years.

Diet

Raccoons are omnivorous and opportunistic. Most of their diet is obtained along shorelines, where the majority of sign is found. They are fond of calorie-rich berries, nuts, and fruits of all types, and in many habitats, vegetation might make up the majority of foods a raccoon eats. Normally solitary, animals may descend on cultivated fields in force, decimating an entire crop. Habituated raccoons also damage fruit trees and grape arbors.

Poorly designed for pursuit, raccoons are consummate scavengers. The carnivorous portion of their diets typically covers the spectrum of invertebrates rather than vertebrates. Crayfish, grasshoppers, beetles, small rodents, frogs, birds, and hatchling turtles are all components of the raccoon's diet. Any animal that can be taken without danger to themselves is prey. Carrion will be eaten but only when fresh.

Raccoons are known for their habit of washing foods at the edges of waterways, a practice alluded to by its species name, *lotor*, which translates as "the washer." The purpose behind this practice is thought to be a sorting process in which sensitive fingerlike toes separate

The track pattern of a raccoon running flat out over hardpack snow; note how forefeet print close together between and behind hind feet—a pattern that legendary tracker Olaus J. Murie called the "Rocking Horse."

inedible matter. Where many animals must swallow small prey whole, a raccoon can pick out the parts it doesn't want.

Mating Habits

Raccoons reach sexual maturity at one year, but males will probably not breed until they first establish their own territories, usually at two years. Mating begins in late January and extends through early March, peaking in February; populations in warm regions may mate in December. Males travel to females from as far away as three miles, attracted by pheromonal scents. Mating is preceded by several days of courtship, during which males den with females. Once impregnated, females reject mates and send them on their way—often to find another receptive female. Female raccoons are believed to take only one mate per breeding season.

Track pattern of a raccoon walking in wet sand; left to right: right front, right hind, left front, left hind, right front.

After a gestation of sixty to seventy days, females retire to a secluded leaf-lined den in a large hollow tree, under its roots, or sometimes in dry culverts, where mothers birth four to eight cubs in April or May. Cubs weigh two ounces at birth and are blind, deaf, and almost naked (altricial). Young open their eyes at three weeks and begin roving around the den. Cubs go outside the den at two months but never stray far from its entrance. At this stage, mothers may move cubs to an alternate den, carrying them one at a time by the nape of the neck. If a predator threatens in the open, the mother pushes her young up a tree and then follows. If cornered, females defend offspring viciously enough to deter even desperate carnivores.

By three months, cubs are weaned and foraging for edible plants and small animals. The family stays together throughout the following winter but separates before the spring mating season, when the mother will probably mate again. Males leave first, seeking their own territories, followed by female siblings who will likely take mates of their own in the coming breeding season.

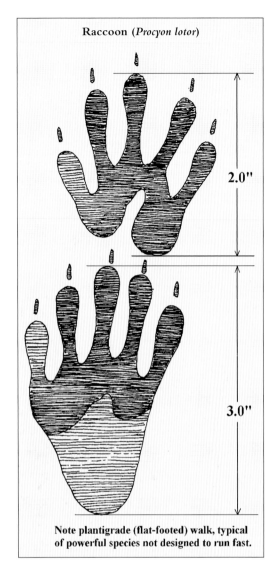

Raccoon (*Procyon lotor*)

2.0"

3.0"

Note plantigrade (flat-footed) walk, typical
of powerful species not designed to run fast.

Behaviorisms

Except for procreational activities, raccoons are solitary and generally nocturnal, but where there are no humans, they may forage along shorelines in daylight. Raccoons aren't true hibernators, but extreme cold or snow may motivate them to hole up (estivate) in a warm den until the weather eases, living off a thick layer of fat and conserving energy. Denned raccoons are normally alone, but mothers and cubs from the previous spring den together, and courting pairs may stay together for a month prior to breeding.

Raccoons have well-developed tactile senses, and research suggests the sensitivity of their fore-paws may be several times that of our own hands. Raccoon paws have the tactility to enable them to snatch submerged foods by feel alone. Handlike forepaws grasp, pull, and tear with sufficient strength to pry open clams and remove the carapaces of cray-fish or even hatchling turtles.

With an ability to grasp branches, raccoons are exceptional climbers. They lack the agility to pursue prey through treetops like a pine marten can, and they climb only to escape enemies or obtain fruit. Raccoons have survived falls of more than thirty feet without injury.

Procyon lotor is a born swimmer that readily takes to water to escape danger. Raccoons rarely swim without purpose, though, because their pelts lack the water-repellent oils contained in the fur of otters or beavers, and their coat becomes saturated.

The left hind (bottom) and left front tracks of a walking raccoon, about one day old.

Family Sciuridae

The squirrel family represents sixty-three species in North America, including marmots, chipmunks, and fox squirrels. *Sciuridae* is Latin for "shade tail," alluding to the long bushy tail of tree squirrels, but ground squirrels like prairie dogs and woodchucks have only a vestigial tail. Family-wide physical characteristics common to all include having four toes on the forefeet and five toes on the hind feet. All are plantigrade hoppers with elongated hind paws that resemble human feet. All are rodents, with chisel-shaped upper and lower incisors that are adapted to gnawing and cutting vegetation.

GRAY SQUIRREL
(*Sciurus carolinensis*)

The most common tree squirrel, with close cousins throughout the Americas, the Gray Squirrel has had no problem coexisting with humans.

The best-known tree squirrels, gray squirrels have been human food for as long as there have been people in North America. In Colonial times, it was common to refer to any long gun smaller than a .45 caliber as a squirrel gun, which infers that squirrel was probably a mainstay of our forebears. Because it is so common, the eastern gray squirrel represents tree squirrels here. The species has close cousins throughout North America, and all share similar diets and traits.

Geographic Range

Sciurus carolinensis occupies the eastern United States to the Mississippi River, as far south as Florida and eastern Texas, and north to the southern edge of Canada. Introduced populations also exist in Italy, Scotland, England, and Ireland, where gray squirrels have thrived to the point of becoming serious pests.

Habitat

Sciurus carolinensis requires a habitat with trees, so it will not be found in prairies, deserts, or places where trees don't provide forage, dens, and escape from predators. Ideal habitat includes nut trees and a variety of ground plants, with close access to water. Larger fox squirrels prefer a mixed habitat of conifers and hardwoods; smaller red squirrels are found in mostly coniferous forests.

Physical Characteristics

Mass: Gray squirrels weigh 1 to 1.5 pounds.

One of the best survivors among tree squirrels, American Gray Squirrels transplanted in the United Kingdom have thrived to the point of becoming pests.

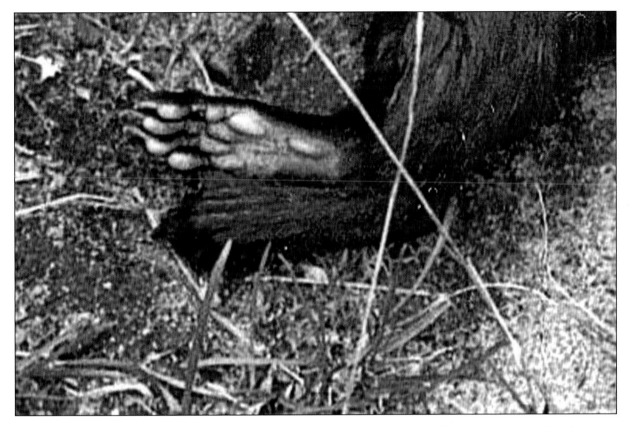

Well-clawed on each of its feet, the acrobatic gray squirrel's elongated hind feet are equipped with long articulated toes for gripping and a knobby sole to maximize surface area and traction.

Body: Squirrels are elongated and furred, with short legs, rounded head, short pointed muzzle, and small round ears. Body length is 16 to 20 inches. There is no difference in body size between genders (dimorphous). Differences in skull size and fur color occur between gray squirrel populations in the northern and southern parts of the species' range. North to south, skull size decreases as a regional adaptation (cline), but mandible sizes and dental arrangements remain the same. Individuals in the South tend more toward a gray coat, while populations in the North are more often black in color.

Tail: The tail is furred and more flat along its top than that of other tree squirrels. Length is 8 to 10 inches—about half the body length. The tail functions as an umbrella in rain or sun and adds insulation for sleeping in cold weather.

Tracks: There are four toes on front feet, five toes on hind. Tracks of front feet are rounded, 1 to 1.5 inches long; hind feet are elongated, 2 to 2.5 inches long. Track pattern is like a rabbit's but has much smaller hind feet prints ahead of forefeet, leaving a pattern like a pair of exclamation points (!!), typical of the hopping gait used by tree squirrels. Total length of track pattern is 7 to 8 inches. Distance between track sets indicates gait: 10 inches for a casual hopping pace, 2 feet at an easy run, 3 feet or more when the animal is fleeing danger.

Scat: Scat is pellets that are dark brown to black, 0.25 inch in diameter. Pellets may exhibit a thin "tail" of undigested plant fibers on one end, indicating fibrous browse. About a dozen pellets are found in a deposit.

Coloration: There are two color phases in *S. carolinensis*. Populations in beech forests tend to have a fur color that matches the trees' gray bark; those living among dark-trunked trees like maples and oaks are mostly black, especially in the North. Black-furred squirrels experience 18 percent less heat loss than gray-colored squirrels in temperatures below freezing, along with a 20 percent lower metabolic rate and a nonshivering (thermogenesis) capacity that's 11 percent higher than in gray individuals. Both color phases exhibit a grizzling of whitish guard hairs along the dorsal parts. Ears and underbelly are often lighter in color than the body. Uncommon, especially in colder latitudes, albino colonies exist in southern Illinois, New Jersey, and South Carolina. The fox squirrel is larger with a reddish pelage; the red squirrel is much smaller, with an orangish coat and white underparts.

Sign: Sign includes beechnut husks and opened acorn, walnut, hickory, and other nuts. In autumn, nut-bearing twigs are snipped from food trees, their cut ends showing a neat, stepped bite from the squirrel's sharp upper and lower incisors. Small patches of loose soil scattered atop forest humus reveal where nuts have been buried for winter storage. In winter, hardpack snow is pocked with holes, about six inches in diameter, where a squirrel burrowed downward to retrieve a nut, leaving a spray of soil atop the snow.

Vocalizations: Chirping barks come from territorial males, especially during the autumn and spring breeding seasons. Alarm calls consist of short clucking barks that humans can imitate by sucking one cheek against their molars. The intensity of a squirrel's alarm is demonstrated by the frequency of the barks: fast chattering means immediate danger; barks become less frequent as the source alarm withdraws.

Life span: Average life span in the wild is about twelve and a half years, but one captive female lived to more than twenty years.

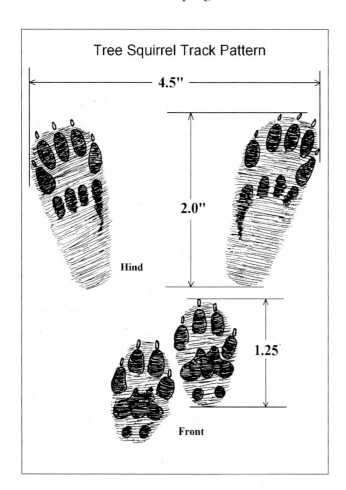

Tree squirrel track pattern as it might appear in snow (gray squirrel shown).

Diet

Nuts and seeds are staples in a gray squirrel's diet, with acorns, chestnuts, and other storable nuts being favored. Tree buds are on the menu in early spring, along with stored nuts that have been frozen in the ground since the previous autumn. In summer the diet includes plants, grasses, and flowers. Pine and cedar nuts and buds are also eaten, and mushrooms are nibbled. Primarily vegetarian, gray and other tree squirrels are known to become carnivorous when plant foods become scarce. Gray squirrels gnaw on deer bones and antlers to wear down constantly growing incisors and to get the minerals they harbor. Wheat and corn are favored foods, making the squirrels a pest species in agricultural areas.

Gray (and fox) squirrels don't remember where every nut is buried, but tree squirrels possess an extraordinary sense of smell that can detect cached nuts under a foot of snow. Not all buried nuts are found, and inevitably more nuts are buried than are eaten. Unretrieved nuts take root, and squirrels help to expand their own habitats by planting trees in places where they wouldn't be otherwise.

Mating Habits

Gray squirrels mate twice each year, once in May through June, and again in December through February. Males older than eleven months are drawn to preestrous females by sexual pheromones a week prior to mating and may travel as far as half a mile. The testes of mating males increase in mass from their non-breeding weight of approximately one gram to as much as seven grams.

Gray Squirrel (*Sciurus carolinensis*)

1.25"

Right Front

1.5"

Right Hind

Tracks as they might appear on firm ground (heel pad of hind foot does not register).

Females may breed at six months, especially where populations are low, but most mate at fifteen months and are fertile for about eight years. Estrus is indicated by an enlarged pink vulva that makes it easier to identify the sexes, which are nearly identical during nonbreeding months. The vulva is typically swollen for eight hours; the vaginal cavity is closed except during estrus.

Territorial battles between mating males are common and noisy, with contenders scrapping furiously on the ground and in the trees. Where populations are high or females are scarce, males have been observed biting off the testicles of competitors. Copulation between pairs is generally over within thirty seconds, and mates then go their separate ways. Males breed with as many partners as possible, but females breed only until they become pregnant. After the female has become impregnated, a mucous plug forms within her vaginal cavity, blocking further entry by sperm and preventing further intercourse.

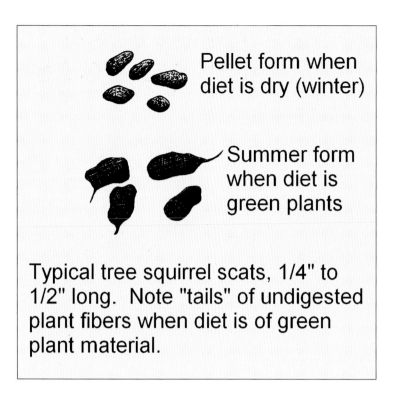

Pellet form when diet is dry (winter)

Summer form when diet is green plants

Typical tree squirrel scats, 1/4" to 1/2" long. Note "tails" of undigested plant fibers when diet is of green plant material.

Gestation averages forty-four days, with two to four kits born in a leaf-lined nest high up inside a hollow tree. Young are born naked (altricial) and whiskered (vibrissal) and weigh four ounces each. Kits nurse constantly for the first seven weeks, and mothers leave them only to eat, drink, and relieve themselves. During her short absences the young may fall prey to raccoons, weasels, and predatory birds that can fit through the den opening. Nursing mothers viciously defend offspring, but mothers never wander far while young are in the suckling stage and may move nursing young to a different nest if it is molested. In cold months nests are in enclosed places, but in warm weather young may be nursed in an open nest of sticks and leaves located on a high tree limb. By ten weeks, squirrel kits are weaned, the family separates, and mothers provide no more care. Adult size and mass are reached at nine months.

Squirrel tracks atop ice that has been dusted with fresh snow show the knobby soles and claws that make tree squirrels so surefooted in their dangerous arboreal habitat.

Behaviorisms

With the exception of nocturnal flying squirrels, tree squirrels are active during daylight (diurnal), with peak activity occurring about two hours after sunrise and two hours prior to sunset. Hot days are spent resting in loafing platforms made from sticks and leaves and located in overhead branches. Unlike maternal nests, loafing platforms are flatter and less concave because they don't contain young that could fall out. Loafing platforms help to determine their builder's age, with those that are more haphazardly constructed usually being made by younger, less-experienced animals.

Male and female gray squirrels are identical in color and size, but an individual's activities can help to identify gender. Males are most active in autumn and spring, when food, territory, and mates make them alert for competitors and more defensive. Females tend to be more active during summer and winter, when they must work to regain energy lost while rearing a litter.

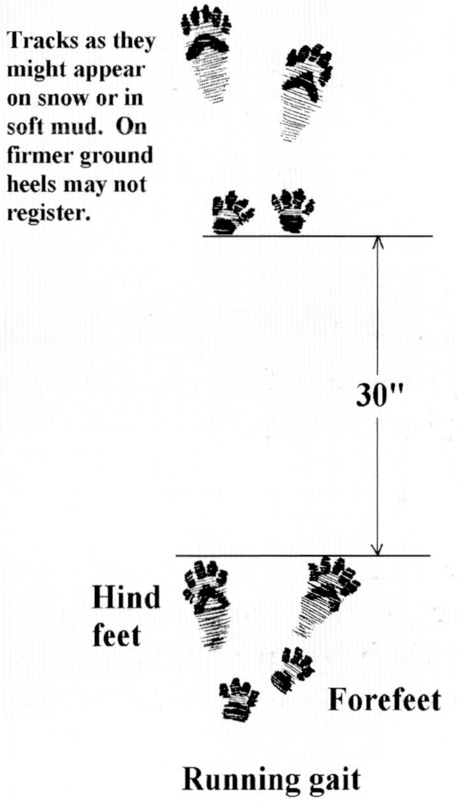

Widely differing estimates have been made of how much acreage can be required to support a healthy gray squirrel; territory size is ultimately determined by availability of resources. A single city block can be home to a half-dozen squirrels so long as sufficient food, water, and nesting sites are available, and in urban parks, where they receive regular handouts from humans, population densities may be higher. Residential areas have proved so attractive to gray squirrels that a pest-removal industry has been created in response to their invasion of attics, garages, and other places where their presence conflicts with humans. The problem is severe among transplanted populations in Great Britain, where gray squirrels are ranked second only to the Norway rat (*Rattus norvegicus*) in terms of property destruction.

Despite being pests in some areas, gray squirrels have a strong following among wildlife enthusiasts, and squirrel-watching has become nearly as popular as bird-watching. Gray and fox squirrels are also very popular with small-game hunters, bringing millions of dollars in revenue to state governments and the sport-hunting industry each year.

Typical tree squirrel running track pattern

Track pattern shown here is typical of all tree squirrel species, and denotes a hopping gait similar to that of rabbits and hares.

Tracks as they might appear on snow or in soft mud. On firmer ground heels may not register.

30"

Hind feet

Forefeet

Running gait

WOODCHUCK
(*Marmota monax*)

Largest of the squirrel family, the woodchuck and its close relatives, the yellow-bellied marmot, hoary marmot, and olympic marmot, are ground-dwelling burrowers that lack the bushy tail associated with tree squirrels. This species gets its common name from the Cree Indian word *woochuk*, which that tribe used to describe all marmots, but the woodchuck retained it because its burrows are most often found near forests.

Best known as the groundhog that emerges from hibernation each year on February 2 to look for its shadow, the woodchuck is the most populous marmot species in North America. Because nearly all of its habits and characteristics are shared by other marmots, the information given here is generally applicable to all species.

Geographic Range

The range of *M. monax* spreads from the Atlantic to the Pacific across North America, extending in a line to the north from New Brunswick, across the southern shore of Hudson Bay, through the Yukon Territory and into central Alaska. Southern boundaries extend from Virginia to Arkansas and northwest to British Columbia. Being burrowers, they will not be found above the Arctic Circle where permafrost prevents digging, although permafrost has been receding for more than a decade, which may in time cause woodchucks to expand their range northward.

Habitat

Like all marmots, woodchucks prefer open areas where they can bask in the sun, but they are never far from the forests that give them their common name. Burrows excavated under the roots of large trees provide protection from digging predators such as bears and wolves, while tall trees permit a quick escape for woodchucks caught by surprise on the ground. High ground with good drainage is a necessity for woodchuck habitat, especially in northern regions that experience potential flooding from snowmelt in spring. Marmots require a source of drinking water nearby, but their excavated dens, which may extend underground as far as 25 feet and have as many as six outlets, must be in earth that remains dry year-round to a depth of at least 5 feet.

Physical Characteristics

Mass: Woodchucks weigh 4.5 to 14 pounds, with the largest individuals occurring in the North. Males are slightly larger and more muscular than females.

Body: They are chunky and stout, with short powerful legs well adapted for digging. Body length is 16 to more than 32 inches. Skull is broad and flat on top, flanked to either side by small roundish ears. The woodchuck's incisors continue to grow throughout its life span, and if they aren't worn down properly, the upper and lower mating pairs can grow past one another (malocclusion), where they may continue to grow until the jawbones are pierced and eating becomes impossible.

Tail: The tail is 3.5 to 9 inches long and well furred but not as bushy as a tree squirrel's; it's about 25 percent of body length.

Tracks: There are four toes on the forefeet, five toes on the hind feet. The rudimentary first digit of the forepaw is covered by a flat nail; the other three digits terminate in curved claws that are useful in digging. The hind foot has five elongated and clawed digits that show clearly in most tracks. Front tracks are about 2 inches long, hind tracks are usually 2.5 inches long but can be 3 inches long or more on soft ground where the entire heel prints. Straddle is 3.5 to 6 inches; walking stride, in which hind feet print on top of or slightly ahead of front tracks, is 3 to 4 inches. In the running stride, which may be as fast as 10 miles per hour, hind feet print ahead of forefeet, which print individually behind and between them; distance between track sets is about 14 inches.

Scat: Scat is elongated and irregular in diameter, usually tapered at one or both ends, with plant fibers in evidence. It is dark brown to black in color, lightening with age. Length is 2 to more than 4 inches.

Coloration: Woodchucks are dark brown to nearly black along the dorsal region and sides, interspersed with coarser guard hairs that are banded with alternating red and yellow, tipped with white. Underbelly is paler, head and feet are much darker. Tail is dark colored, much shorter in comparison to that of tree squirrels. There is one molt from late May to September, which begins at the tail and progresses forward. The feet are black and plantigrade. The woodchuck's long incisors are white or nearly white, lacking the dark-yellow pigmentation of other large rodents like porcupines or beavers.

Sign: Burrow entrances 10 to 14 inches in diameter are dug into knolls and hillsides, sometimes beneath the roots of standing trees, and occasionally into and under a hole in the trunk of a standing hollow tree. The woodchuck also possesses three nipple–anal (perineal) scent glands that secrete a musky odor, and trees, stumps, or other prominent objects around den entrances will often be scented.

Vocalizations: Woodchucks are often vocal, particularly when alarmed, which explains its nickname "whistle-pig." The alarm cry is a single, loud, shrill whistle, often preceded by a squirrel-like bark. The call used to attract mates, to warn intruders impinging on its territory, or from mothers calling young to the safety of the burrow is a loud whistle followed by a less-piercing call and ending with a series of softer whistles that cannot be heard except at close range. Teeth grinding, chattering, and even doglike growls are common when woodchucks are cornered by a predator.

Life span: There is a high attrition rate for young, but woodchucks live up to six years in the wild and up to ten years in captivity.

Diet

Woodchucks are mostly herbivorous, preferring clovers, alfalfa, plantains, and grasses during the summer months but also bark and buds of wild cherry, sumac, and other shrubs in early spring, before food plants are available. Poplar, cottonwood, and aspens are of particular importance because they provide food in the form of bark, buds, and leaves throughout the woodchuck's active time of year. Woodchucks will also eat an occasional bird egg, grasshopper, snail, or tree frog and probably the young of most small rodents, but these minor predations appear to be opportunistic in nature. Marmots aren't known to eat carrion, but they will gnaw shed antlers and bones for the nutrients they contain.

Because the woodchuck's range and habitat encompass most of the richest farming areas in North America, this species more than any other marmot has incurred the wrath of farmers. Lands cleared for planting provide good habitat, and crops like alfalfa, clover, wheat, and especially corn are relished by woodchucks that can eat in excess of one and a half pounds per animal per day, breaking down and killing plants while they feed.

In late summer, the woodchucks feed more urgently. Each animal needs to gain about 25 percent of its body weight in a layer of fat that will insulate and sustain it through the winter. During this predenning period, a woodchuck becomes especially territorial and protective of its food resources. Trespassers, especially yearlings wandering in search of their own territories, will be driven off as plants become scarcer with shortening days.

Mating Habits

Breeding occurs in early spring, usually within two weeks after woodchucks emerge from hibernation in late March or April. Adults are normally solitary, but the territories of adult males typically overlap those of several females. This arrangement permits established males to make contact with receptive females without trespassing onto the territories of other males. When two males do compete, the battles consist of boxing matches in which both contenders stand erect on hind feet, slapping and biting one another until one withdraws.

Females are monoestrous, accepting only one mate per breeding season. Males stay in their mate's dens for about one week—the only time these normally solitary animals are social—before leaving to seek out another female. After a gestation period of approximately thirty-two days, females give birth to litters of one to nine naked and blind young, with five being the average litter size, in April or May. Newborns weigh about 26 grams and measure about 4 inches long.

Females have four pairs of teats and nurse their young from a standing position, staying with them almost constantly for their first two weeks of life. At three weeks, the young begin crawling about inside the den, and at four weeks they open their eyes. By five weeks, the young woodchucks are fully active and begin exploring for short distances around the den entrance, scurrying back inside if the mother issues an alarm whistle.

Young woodchucks are weaned at six weeks but may remain with their mother until July or August, when she forces them to disperse. Yearlings must find or excavate their own burrows after leaving their mothers and will hibernate alone in their first winter. Females will probably mate on emerging from their dens the following spring, but competition may force young males to wait until the next spring, after they've established their own territories.

Behaviorisms

Woodchucks are the most solitary marmot species, and both genders are generally hostile toward one another on meeting (agonistic). Battles are usually of short duration and relatively bloodless, but established adults do not tolerate trespassers. Reports of individuals sharing a den stem from observations made during the short mating period when males occupy the dens of their mates or of nearly grown offspring denning with their mother.

Woodchucks are most often observed during the day, but they may become partly nocturnal if harassed by humans. The stereotypical image of this species is an animal standing erect, forelimbs held tightly to the front of its body, as it surveys the surrounding area. Standing upright is an alert posture, but woodchucks prefer to spend their time on all fours as they feed, sunbathe, and comb their fur, never far from the den entrance. If alarmed, a woodchuck retreats into its den, turning to face outward once inside. This is a defensive position from which the marmot can bite and claw with surprising ferocity. The sharp incisors of a defensive woodchuck persuade most predators to seek easier prey, but bears, badgers, and wolves can dig to the main chamber, forcing the occupant to try to escape through one of up to five escape tunnels. Woodchucks are less agile than their tree squirrel cousins but can climb trees to escape predators.

The woodchuck is a true hibernator, spending the cold winter months in a comalike slumber within a grass-lined sleeping chamber deep inside its den. The animals enter the den to stay prior to the first permanent snowfall, usually in late November in the North and in December in the southern part of the species' range. Once inside and asleep, the marmot's body undergoes remarkable physiological changes: Its body temperature falls from a normal 97°F to 40°F, and its heart rate slows from about 100 beats per minute to just four beats per minute. It remains in this state until warming days cause it to emerge in April, although its deep slumber appears to become lighter as spring approaches. The animals do not ritually leave their dens to see if they cast a shadow on February 2, but the annual Groundhog Day festival held in Punxsutawney, Pennsylvania, creates enough commotion to awaken a hibernating woodchuck. This bit of American folklore, which coincides with Candlemas Day, is rooted in an Old World belief that sunny skies, which allowed the European badger (*Meles meles*) to see its shadow, heralded another six weeks of winter.

Family Erethizontidae

The family of porcupines is represented throughout the world, which demonstrates the effectiveness of their common defensive weapon (the family name, *Erethizon*, is Latin for "one who rises in anger"). All are slow-moving rodents that have adapted to ward off predators with the hard modified hairs interspersed in the fur on their backs and tails. These "quills" are essentially sharp needles tipped with minute barbs. Because predators have almost universally evolved to kill food animals through hard physical contact using teeth and claws, these quills provide porcupines with a shield that can inflict serious and sometimes fatal injuries to attackers. A carnivore with a mouthful of embedded quills cannot eat, and it does not have the means to extract them, and most predators will suffer a serious infection.

PORCUPINE
(*Erethizon dorsatum*)

The single species of North American porcupine has been worshipped and hated by humans, protected in some states, persecuted in others. Many a hungry woodsman, including members of the Lewis and Clark Expedition, has blessed the porcupine for being the only prey he could run down and safely dispatch with a club (a hard blow across the nose usually kills it instantly).

In some places, the porcupine's value as survival food is superseded by its importance as a pest. Commercially valuable pines, particularly white pines, are favored winter foods, and porcupines frequently kill mature trees by eating the young bark from tops and saplings. Rural homeowners dislike that the porcupine's love for salt causes it to gnaw perspiration-soaked wooden tool handles and even the varnish on wooden house siding. Corn crops and orchard trees may also be damaged, but female porcupines produce only one offspring per year, keeping agricultural damage low and making populations easy to control. Evoking the most emotion are pet injuries that make even some veterinarians say they hate porcupines. In spite of prejudice toward live porcupines, Native American–made "quill boxes" crafted from bark and dyed quills fetch hundreds of dollars apiece.

Geographic Range

The common porcupine is native to boreal North America from Alaska and across Canada south of the Arctic Circle to Labrador. Its range covers the western half of the United States, southward from Montana through New Mexico, and into northern Mexico. In the eastern half of the United States, porcupines are found only in the northernmost forested regions,

With its large, low-slung bulk, the porcupine might not appear to be much of a climber, but long claws mated to articulated fingerlike toes make it one of the best tree climbers in the animal world.

covering most of New England, northern Michigan, northern Wisconsin, and northeast Minnesota.

Habitat

Porcupines are found primarily in coniferous forests but may spend part of the year in deciduous woods, especially in spring, when trees are budding. Preferred habitat is mixed forest of pine, deciduous hardwoods and softwoods, and a variety of ground plants, and nearly every environment will include tall trees and a source of freshwater nearby. There have been reports of porcupines frequenting riparian (riverfront) areas in mountainous regions and even denning in rock crevices, but they prefer woodlands that provide food, shelter, and refuge from enemies.

Physical Characteristics

Mass: Porcupines weigh 8 to 40 pounds, with the largest specimens occurring in the North.

Body: They are rodentlike, with humped back and short legs. Dorsal region, especially the tail, is covered with coarse hairs and approximately 30,000 hollow, barbed quills that can be voluntarily detached on contact but not thrown. The longest quills occur on the rump and tail, and the shortest are on the neck; there are no quills on the underbelly. Body length is 25 to 37 inches. Head is small in proportion to body and round, with short muzzle, flat face, and small round ears. Prominent yellow-orange incisors must be kept from growing past one another (malocclusion) through constant gnawing.

Tail: The tail is large, round, and clublike, with the top side heavily covered with quills. Length is 6 to 12 inches.

Tracks: There are four toes on forefeet, five toes on hind feet. Toes are long and articulated, each tipped with a heavy, slightly curved claw 0.5 to nearly 1 inch long. Front track is 2 to 3 inches long, including claws; hind track is 3 to 4.5 inches long, including claws. Tracks elongated and plantigrade (flat-footed), with distinctive pebble-textured soles. At a walk, the porcupine's usual gait, hind prints register ahead of fore prints, occasionally overlapping. In snow the porky's wide, low-slung belly often drags, leaving a trough that can obscure tracks. In sand, tracks may be brushed by the heavy tail, which typically swings back and forth, leaving striated broomlike markings.

Scat: In winter, scat is curved pellets with a sawdust-like texture, much like the muskrat's but not connected lengthwise. Pellets are dark brown, each about 1 inch long, and usually distinguishable by a uniquely porcupine groove running lengthwise along the inside radius. In spring, when the porcupine's diet changes to succulent green plants, pellets are often shorter, with more-squared ends, sometimes connected by grass fibers like a string of beads. Other forms seen from spring through autumn include formless blobs, with undigested plant fibers.

Revered as a survival food for humans stranded in a wilderness, the porcupine is disliked by farmers and cabin owners for its fondness of the salt found in treated wood and perspiration-soaked tool handles.

Almost beautiful to look at, the porcupine is considered a pest by timber companies because it eats the bark of young pines in the winter.

Coloration: Most porcupines are covered with coarse gray hairs, but some may be brown or even black. The unquilled belly is lighter in color than the back and sides. Hollow quills are black tipped with white.

Sign: Most obvious are the porcupine's winter gnawing of smooth-barked pines, especially near the trees' tops, leaving irregular patches of exposed wood. In winter look for scattered twig ends lying under large pines that serve as food sources (red squirrels also nip off cone-bearing twigs from spruces and hemlocks). Den openings at the base of hollow trees may have accumulations of scat pellets about their entrances. Bones and antlers are gnawed to obtain the minerals in them, leaving gouges much larger than those made by smaller squirrels. Porcupines also gnaw processed lumber, especially wood that has been treated with varnish, which they eat for its salt content.

Vocalizations: Porcupines are usually silent, even when cornered. Most vocalizations are heard during the autumn mating season, when males may grunt, squeak, and sometimes snort while in pursuit of mates.

Life span: They live up to eight years.

Diet

The porcupine is entirely vegetarian. In spring, before ground plants sprout, the animals climb high into poplar and aspen trees, especially, to feed on fleshy buds; buds of willow, staghorn sumac, beech, and others are also eaten. The animals prefer green plants, including grasses and sedges, plantains, beechnuts, cresses, mustard, chicory, and dandelions. As summer progresses, the diet changes to include ripening fruits, particularly apples.

When winter makes ground plants unavailable, porcupines feed on bark stripped from sumac, willows, and dogwoods, but they also climb into tall trees to reach tender bark and

The right front foot of this porcupine shows the unique pebbled texture of its soles.

twig ends. White pines are a favorite, and a large tree may be occupied by a porcupine for more than a week. They also eat wood that has traces of salt, including sweat-soaked tool handles, plywood boats, decks, and wooden siding or shingles. Legendary tracker Olaus J. Murie once described how he was forced to restrain a half dozen porcupines that persisted in gnawing his canoe by looping cord around their necks and tying them to a tree until morning.

Mating Habits

Female porcupines may mate at six months of age, but competition usually prevents males from breeding until eighteen months. The males' testes descend into scrotal pouches between late August and early September, and production of sperm cells (spermatogenesis) peaks during October. Mating occurs October through November, and during sixty days of breeding, males may travel several miles to pursue mates. It's during this time that normally silent porcupines are likely to be vocal, especially when several males pursue a single female into a large tree. Males are rarely violent toward one another, but arboreal pursuits can turn dangerous if a shoving and nipping match causes one of them to fall. Females are passive, attracting males with pheromonal scents but concentrating mostly on eating in preparation for pregnancy. Male courtship rituals include squeaking, grunting, a hopping dance, tree-borne contests of strength, and urinating onto the female. Females are in estrus for twelve hours, so mating is urgent and brief. If a female fails to become pregnant within that period, she will come into heat again (polyestrous) in another twenty-five to thirty days.

A long-standing jocular answer to the question of just how spiny porcupines engage in sex has been "carefully," but in fact, mating occurs in the same manner as with other animals. When the female is ready, she voluntarily pulls the quills along her back downward and holds them flat against her body, then raises her tail over her back, exposing the unquilled genitalia. The male then mounts her in conventional fashion. Once she is impregnated, a mucous plug forms in the female porcupine's vaginal cavity to prevent further entry by sperm, and she loses interest in mating. Her mate, who might have come from several miles distant, will set out to find another receptive female before the breeding period ends, and he takes no part in the rearing of offspring.

The gestation period spans thirty weeks, which is very long for a small mammal and probably includes a period of delayed implantation. Pregnant females give birth to a single pup (twins are rare) in April or May within a den usually located inside a standing hollow tree, sometimes in a rock crevice. Young are precocial, born fully quilled and with eyes open, but quills are soft and do not harm the mother. After being exposed to open air for about one hour, the quills harden, and the youngster becomes a smaller duplicate of its mother.

In captivity, mother porcupines have suckled their young for periods spanning several months, but youngsters in the wild are able to subsist on vegetation within two weeks. Adolescents as young as one month are capable of caring for themselves, although young porcupines accompany their mothers for five months or more; young females may even mate with the same male as their mothers breed with. Males wander off in search of their own territories during their first summer.

Porcupine populations rise and fall in twelve-year cycles; a typical cycle consists of two years of decline, followed by a rise over the next ten years.

Behaviorisms

Porcupines are normally solitary and rarely show territorial aggression. In harsh weather, several individuals may take shelter in the same hollow tree, cave, or culvert, but when fair weather returns, they resume solitary lifestyles. Porcupines do not hibernate, but pregnant females especially seek out birthing dens. Dens are used regularly throughout the winter, and there may be several throughout a territory.

The entrance to a porcupine den is marked with scat pellets, sometimes a small mountain of them if the den has been used for several years. When the den is within a hollow standing tree, there will usually be a ledge inside, 10 feet or more above its base, where the animal sleeps. This platform is often partially or entirely constructed of scat pellets compressed

Porcupine scat is generally a curved pellet, about a quarter-inch in diameter, often with a longitudinal groove along a pellet's inside radius that is seen in no other species (muskrats have similar scats, but no groove). Darker scat to the left is from a small whitetail.

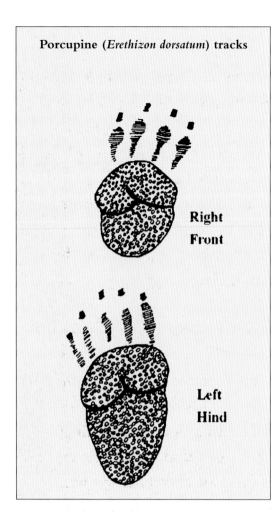

Porcupine (*Erethizon dorsatum*) tracks

Right Front

Left Hind

by weight to a hard surface. Above this elevated platform, a small observation hole will be gnawed through the tree's shell, and trackers can often spot a porcupine peering out at them.

On hot days, porcupines escape biting flies and the heat on a thick, shaded branch high up in a tree, where they are revealed as an uncharacteristic large bump. The heavily quilled tail and rump habitually point toward the tree's trunk, the direction from which most dangers approach. This defensive position frustrates bobcats and most climbing carnivores, but the fisher can clamber past the porcupine along the underside of the branch to emerge in front of it, gaining access to the unprotected head.

Porcupines prefer to forage at night, emerging at sunset from dens and sleeping trees to forage. If a hungry or inexperienced predator threatens, the porcupine points its tail end toward the enemy, turning with the predator to keep its most potent armament positioned for a spiny slap. Given an opportunity, the porcupine will escape by climbing a tree.

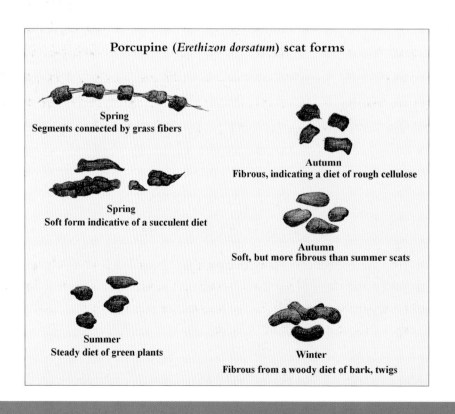

Porcupine (*Erethizon dorsatum*) scat forms

Spring
Segments connected by grass fibers

Spring
Soft form indicative of a succulent diet

Summer
Steady diet of green plants

Autumn
Fibrous, indicating a diet of rough cellulose

Autumn
Soft, but more fibrous than summer scats

Winter
Fibrous from a woody diet of bark, twigs

Family Leporidae

This is the family of rabbits and hares. Rabbits (genus *Sylvilagus*) are sometimes confused with hares (genus *Lepus*), but rabbits are generally smaller, with shorter ears and shorter legs. Faster running hares are more prone to open areas, while rabbits prefer brushy habitats where they can hide. Hares give birth to fully furred young in relatively open places, while rabbit newborns are born naked in a sheltering burrow and require a longer period of maternal care. Both are prolific breeders, with reproductive rates adapted to offset predation from numerous carnivores.

Rabbits and hares are not rodents but belong to the order Lagomorpha, a group that includes the diminutive pikas. Unlike rodents, lagomorphs have a second, smaller pair of incisor teeth directly behind the chisel-like upper incisors. This dental arrangement gives teeth a very sharp scissorlike cutting action, enabling them to chop tough cellulose into fine pieces that digest more easily. Lagomorphs are also remarkable in that males carry their scrotum ahead of the penis, instead of behind it, a characteristic otherwise seen only in marsupials.

Worldwide, there are eighty species of lagomorphs, categorized in thirteen genera, grouped into two families: Leporidae (rabbits and hares) and Ochotonidae (pikas). Native populations of lagomorphs are found on all continents except Antarctica, southern South America, and Australia. (In Australia, introduced lagomorphs have thrived to the point of becoming pests.)

SNOWSHOE HARE
(*Lepus americanus*)

Known as the varying hare because individuals in the North grow a white coat in winter, the snowshoe gets its common name from oversized hind feet that give it flotation on deep snow and mud. One of the smallest hares, the snowshoe jackrabbit is a vital food source for many carnivores, especially the lynx and bobcat.

The snowshoe hare hasn't quite changed into its white winter coat, which has been grizzled brown all summer. (Photo coutrtesy USFWS.)

Geographic Range

Snowshoe hares inhabit the northern United States, from New England through New York, Michigan, northern Wisconsin, northern Minnesota, and northern North Dakota. To the south, their range extends only along mountain ranges that are snow covered in winter, to northern California along the Cascade Mountains, to Colorado along the Rockies, and through West Virginia and Virginia along the Allegheny and Appalachian mountain ranges. To the north, snowshoes inhabit nearly all of Canada and Alaska south of the Arctic Circle. The snowshoe hare's northern range reaches, but seldom overlaps, that of the arctic hare (*Lepus arcticus*), with a precise demarcation between the ranges of either species.

Habitat

While rabbits tend toward thickets to hide them from danger, snowshoe hares prefer more open areas where they can rely on powerful hindquarters and large feet to launch them beyond reach of predators at speeds exceeding 25 miles per hour. Secluded bogs, marshes, and swamps are preferred during daylight hours, but at night the hares venture out to feed in more open areas, such as meadows, shorelines, and roadside ditches.

Physical Characteristics

Mass: Snowshoes weigh 2 to more than 4 pounds, less than half the weight of larger hare species; it is about the same weight as an eastern cottontail rabbit, with which the snowshoe shares much of its range.

Body: The body is rabbitlike, with a humped back, long powerful hind legs, and long and wide hind feet. Body length is 15 to 21 inches. Snowshoes have a round head, blunt muzzle, and large eyes at either side of the head. Ears are 3 inches long, shorter than most other hares, to minimize heat loss. Males (bucks) are slightly smaller than females (does)—unusual among mammals but typical among leporids.

Tail: The tail is dark gray or black on top, whitish below, and 1 to 2 inches long.

Tracks: There are four toes on front and hind feet. Forefeet are comparatively round, 1.5 to 2 inches long; hind feet are very large, 3 to 4.5 inches long. In winter, tracks may be obscured by heavy fur around the pads. At a casual hop, hind feet register ahead of forefeet, leaving a track pattern that looks like paired exclamation points (!!), similar to that of a tree squirrel but several times larger. At a relaxed hop, a set of all four tracks measures 10 to 16 inches. Distance between track sets may be more than 15 feet, with longer leaps denoting a faster pace.

Scat: Scat is typical of rabbits and hares: marble- or egg-shaped pellets. Diameter is about 0.5 inch. Color is usually dark brown when fresh, becoming lighter colored and more sawdustlike with age. Scat pellets are generally found in groups of a half dozen or more. Note that rabbits and hares have a digestive process called "cecal fermentation," in which rough cellulose is eaten, pooped out in the form of green spheres, then reeaten, redigested, and finally excreted as brown, fully digested pellets. A tracker who finds green pellets can presume that their owner was frightened away.

This snowshoe hare demonstrates the effectiveness of its white winter coat. (Photo courtesy National Park Service.)

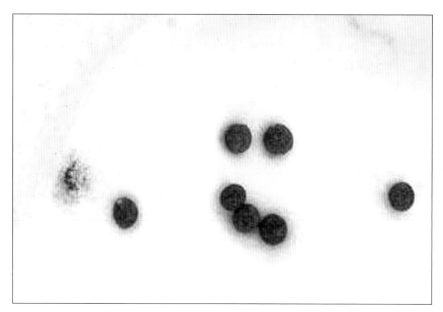

Hare and rabbit scats are generally spherical, about a half-inch in diameter, first excreted as green pellets (brown in winter, when diets consist of dry, woody bark and twigs), then re-ingested and excreted a second time as brown balls from which all nutrients have been extracted. This process is called cecal fermentation.

Coloration: The snowshoe is brown in summer, becoming grizzled with age, with a darker dorsal line and longer fur than the cottontail. It has a whitish belly, brown face, black ear tips, and often a white patch on top of the head. In snow country the coat turns entirely white except for black ear tips. Snowshoes in Washington and Oregon seldom undergo this photoperiodic color change, remaining brown all year. In New York's Adirondack Mountains, there is a population that remains black (melanistic) all year. Winter molts begin in November as patchy white spots that become larger until the animal is completely white, a process that takes about seventy days. Snowshoes possess two separate sets of hair follicles—one that grows only white hairs, others growing brown and gray hairs. Color changes are regulated by daylight, not temperature, and warm winters can result in white hares that contrast starkly against snowless ground.

Sign: In winter, sign includes stripped, bark-less shrubs like sumac, dogwood, and willow. Neatly clipped grasses and stems are seen in summer. Trails are often regularly used and well packed; trails in snow may be trenches more than a foot deep, enabling hares to run fast through troughs too narrow for predators to use.

Vocalizations: Hares are normally silent. Mothers purr while nursing; newborns whimper and whine; the alarm cry is a prolonged squeal. In all cases the calls of hares are lower toned than those of a rabbit. When battling over territory, combatants growl and hiss. Thumping a hind foot repeatedly against the earth is both an alarm and a ploy to entice hidden predators into revealing themselves.

Life span: Few snowshoe hares die of old age; most become prey to a host of predators. Average life span is four years.

Diet

The snowshoe hare's diet is broadly varied but normally vegetarian, including grasses, vetches, asters, jewelweed, strawberry, pussytoes, dandelions, clovers, and horsetails. In winter, snowshoes forage on buds, twigs, smooth bark, and the tips of evergreen twigs. If plant foods are scarce, they have been known to raid traps baited for carnivores to get meat.

A notable trait among leporids is their need to eat the same food twice. Much of the hare's diet is tough cellulose, and because most of the hare's digestive processes are contained in the lower gut, foods must be eaten, excreted, then reeaten to extract all available nutrients. Called "cecal fermentation," this process permits the hare to quickly ingest plants where feeding may be hazardous; then the hare can retire to a safe location where the plants can be completely digested at leisure.

Although considered food by most carnivores, snowshoes are good survivors, a trait that can be seen in the lack of fat on their bodies. With a broad diet that encompasses most vegetation, as well as carrion when times get hard, the hares have little need to carry food reserves on their bodies. But they do need to maintain a lean and muscular body that can outrun fast predators such as the coyote. Early frontiersmen for whom hares and rabbits were a winter staple often suffered from "rabbit starvation" by winter's end. Fat malnutrition occurs—as it did with the Lewis and Clark Expedition—when fat is lacking in the diet, even when plenty of other foods are available.

Mating Habits

Breeding season encompasses the summer months, beginning in March, when testicles descend, and extending through August, when testicles retract and go dormant. Males pursue females by their pheromonal scents, frequently congregating around receptive does in groups.

Snowshoe hare
(*Lepus americanus*)

Snowshoe, or Varying, Hare in its all-white winter coat. Snowshoe hares in southern latitudes may remain brown all year.

Mating contests between males resemble boxing matches: Both contenders rise on their hind legs and bat at one another with sharp-clawed forefeet. If one is knocked onto its back, powerful hind legs kick and scratch. Despite their apparent ferocity, these battles end quickly and are seldom injurious to either party.

Snowshoe does are polyestrous, coming into heat whenever they aren't pregnant throughout the summer months, and both genders engage in sex with any available mate (polygynandrous). This lascivious behavior ensures that these prolific breeders have a strong and varied gene pool.

Gestation takes thirty-five days, with litters of two to eight fully furred precocial young being birthed in a nest atop the ground, sometimes in an unoccupied burrow. Newborns are able to run within two hours of birth and begin feeding on vegetation within twenty-four hours. Mothers nurse litters for thirty days and are likely to be pregnant again before they are weaned. Does may birth as many as four litters per summer, and newborn females may mate as soon as they've been weaned. This rapid reproduction rate makes snowshoes resistant to predation from the many meat eaters that hunt it, and it's unlikely that snowshoe hares will become endangered.

This snowshoe hare was traveling at an easy hop; note that forefeet print close together and behind more widely-spaced hind feet.

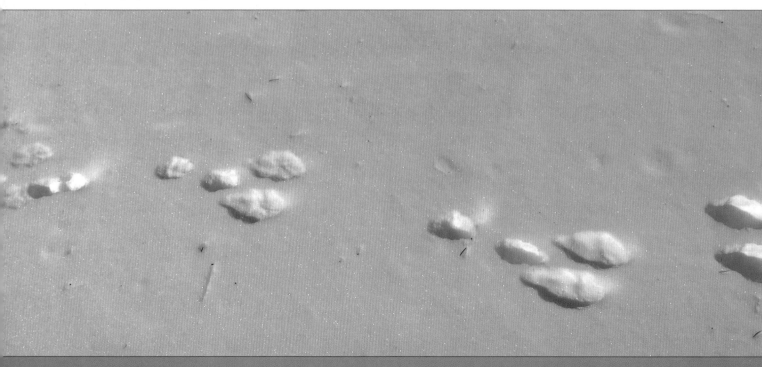

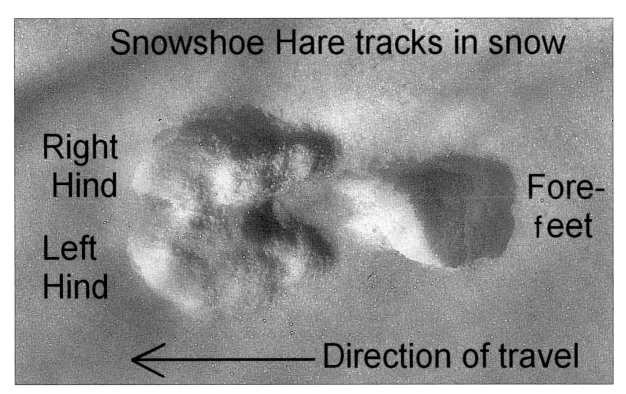

Snowshoe Hare tracks in snow

Right
Hind

Left
Hind

Fore-
feet

← —————— Direction of travel

Behaviorisms

Snowshoe hares are solitary, but dense populations may force them to live together. Normally, an adult's territory may encompass up to 18 acres, but when populations peak, territories may shrink to a fraction of that size. Actual population densities may range from one to as many as 10,000 individuals per square mile, with numbers typically increasing for nine years,

then drastically falling off in the tenth. Sudden population declines appear to be normal for this species and include epidemics of pneumonia, fungal infections, salmonella, and tularemia. At the root of these plaguelike illnesses is malnutrition brought on by depletion of food resources. A secondary effect of the snowshoe's cyclic decline is a sudden decrease in populations of the lynx, which relies heavily on hares in its own diet, one year later.

The greatest fluctuations in snowshoe hare populations occur in northwestern Canada, and the least occur in Colorado's Rocky Mountains. Reasons include greater diversity among predator and prey species in warmer regions, while colder climates tend to be less varied, and relationships

Hares and rabbits serve as food to many predators—like this gray wolf on Lake Superior's Isle Royale—and their prodigious reproductive rates reflect that. (Photo courtesy National Parks Service.)

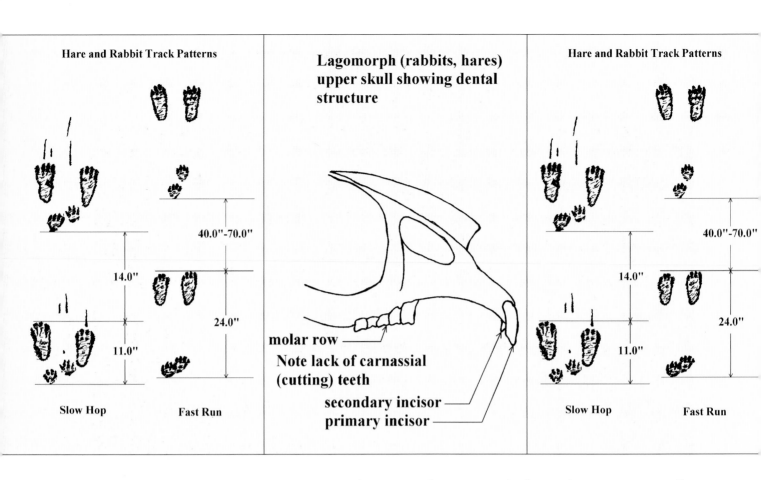

Lagomorph (rabbits, hares) upper skull showing dental structure

40.0"-70.0"

14.0"

11.0"

24.0"

Slow Hop

Fast Run

molar row
Note lack of carnassial (cutting) teeth
secondary incisor
primary incisor

40.0"-70.0"

14.0"

11.0"

24.0"

Slow Hop

Fast Run

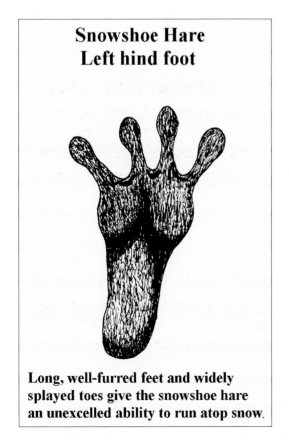

Snowshoe Hare
Left hind foot

Long, well-furred feet and widely splayed toes give the snowshoe hare an unexcelled ability to run atop snow.

between hunter and hunted more critically symbiotic.

When a hare runs from danger, it zigzags through underbrush at high speed, changing direction constantly to make itself hard to follow. Hares rely on a maze of trails, each scented with frequent scat deposits, to confuse the most acute sense of smell. Snowshoes must escape quickly because they tire after a few hundred yards, while many enemies can maintain top running speed for more than a mile. When it begins to tire, a hare freezes and remains motionless, hoping to go unnoticed by its pursuer. If open water is nearby, a hare in imminent danger will probably try to swim from a predator.

On warm summer evenings, snowshoe hares may be seen rolling about on gravel road shoulders. These dust baths loosen shedding fur and help to dislodge fleas and mites. The animals sometimes engage in this behavior in early morning, but most dust baths are taken in the evening because the majority of parasites are contracted while sleeping during the daylight hours.

EASTERN COTTONTAIL RABBIT
(*Sylvilagus floridanus*)

Able to breed continuously the year round, cottontail rabbits are a critical source of food for most American predators wherever they are found.

Immortalized by fables and songs, cottontails are the most widespread rabbit in North America. Like all rabbits, it differs from hares by having shorter, more rounded ears, a smaller body, and shorter hind legs. The cottontail is a fast short-distance sprinter that prefers to elude enemies in thick cover, rather than outrunning them across open terrain. Because it is so common, and because its traits, behaviorisms, and diet are typical of rabbits, it has been selected to represent the genus *Sylvilagus*.

Geographic Range

Cottontails are the most widely distributed rabbits in North America. To the north, the species ranges into southern Manitoba and Quebec. Except for Maine, it occupies all of the eastern United States from the Atlantic coast to North Dakota, south to Texas, through Mexico and into Central America and northwestern South America. To the west, cottontails inhabit the Rocky Mountains from Mexico through eastern Arizona and into Nevada.

Habitat

Supremely adaptable, the eastern cottontail is at home in any environment that provides water and cover in which to hide, including deserts, swamps, coniferous and deciduous

In winter, when green plants become unavailable, cottontails consume bark and twigs; note the neat stepped cut of this green twig, created by the scissor action of the rabbit's upper and lower incisors.

forests, and rainforests. Currently, the eastern cottontail seems to prefer edge environments between woods and open terrain, including meadows, orchards and farmlands, hedgerows, and clear-cut forests with young trees and brush. The eastern cottontail's range extends into that of six other rabbits and six species of hares, although, like all rabbits, it prefers less-open terrain than hares.

Physical Characteristics

Mass: Cottontails weigh 2 to more than 4 pounds.

Body: They have a high rounded back, ears that are 2 to 3 inches long, muscular flanks, and long hind feet. Head is rounded, with short muzzle, flat face, and large eyes at either side. Body length is 14 to 18 inches.

Tail: The tail is brown on top, fluffy cotton-white below. Length is 1.5 to 2.5 inches.

Tracks: There are four toes on all four feet. Fore prints are round, 1 to 1.5 inches long. Hind feet are elongated, 3 to 4 inches long. Claws show in clear tracks. Toes are generally not splayed like a snowshoe hare's.

Scat: Scat is spherical pellets, sometimes flattened discs, usually less than 0.5 inch in diameter. Color is green to dark brown (see Diet section), becoming lighter with age. Pellets are deposited in groups of six or more.

Coloration: The brown coat is interspersed with gray and black guard hairs and is uniform over back, sides, top of tail, and head, except for a reddish patch on the nape of the neck. Ears are black tipped; the underside is buff colored. Cottontails undergo two molts per

Cottontail scat is largely indiscernible from that of the snowshoe hare, except that the usually spherical pellets are slightly smaller, at just under half an inch.

Sometimes mistaken for rodents, rabbits and hares are actually lagomorphs, with a second pair of incisors located directly behind the primary incisors in the upper jaw.

year: The spring molt occurs from mid-April to mid-July, leaving a short brown summer coat; from mid-September through October, the brown pelage is shed and replaced by a warmer grayish winter coat.

Sign: Sign includes neatly nipped-off flower and plant stems. Shrubs stripped of bark down to the cambium layer show where rabbits browsed in winter. Oblong "forms" of compressed grasses, snow, and sand show where a rabbit lay for an extended period while resting or sleeping. Disturbances on graveled road shoulders show where a rabbit took a dust bath to dislodge parasites and shed fur.

Vocalizations: A bleating distress call is intended to startle a predator into hesitating. Bucks (males) chatter and squeal loudly during and immediately after copulation. Nursing does purr while suckling young and sometimes emit a sharp alarm bark if an intruder approaches.

Life span: Cottontails live up to five years but usually less than two years because of heavy predation.

Diet

The cottontail is herbivorous, with roughly 50 percent of its summer diet consisting of grasses, and the balance is composed of a broad variety of ground plants. Its double row of upper incisors chop tough cellulose fibers into fine clippings that digest more easily. In winter the cottontail's diet turns to woody browse and bark. Deepening snows actually work for the rabbits by enabling them to reach bark and twigs that were previously inaccessible, and their gnawing makes them a pest to orchard farmers. Typical of lagomorphs, tough plant materials are digested by a process called cecal fermentation, a variation of the cud-chewing process of ruminant species. With cecal fermentation, ingested plant material is partially digested as it passes through the digestive system and is expelled from the anus as green pellets. The predigested pellets are then reeaten and pass through the digestive tract a second time, where cellulose is broken down and nutrients extracted completely. Like cud chewing, this permits rabbits to quickly eat plant foods in places that may be dangerous for them and then retire to complete the digestive process in seclusion.

Cottontails may forage at any time in places where they feel safe. In summer, they sleep away the day in cool underground burrows, sometimes in brush piles, but increased calorie needs in winter often force them to forage at all hours. In every season, activities are normally crepuscular, peaking in the first three hours after sunrise and again in the twilight hours.

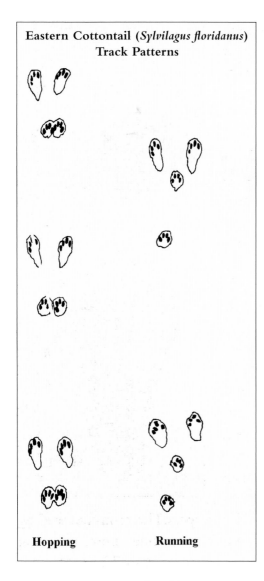

Eastern Cottontail (*Sylvilagus floridanus*)
Track Patterns

Hopping   **Running**

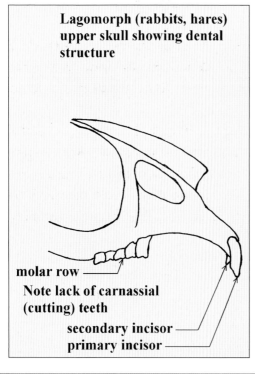

Lagomorph (rabbits, hares) upper skull showing dental structure

molar row ———
Note lack of carnassial (cutting) teeth
secondary incisor ———
primary incisor ———

Mating Habits

Serving as food for so many carnivores has given cottontails extraordinary reproductive abilities. Individuals reach sexual maturity by three months of age, and 25 percent of the rabbits born in summer will be the offspring of juveniles less than six months old. The start of mating season coincides with the spring molt, triggered by lengthening days (photoperiodic), warming temperatures, and the availability of green foods. Bucks, whose testicles are retracted during winter, become sexually ready in mid-February, although does don't come into estrus until mid-March.

This interval gives adult males a period in which to find prospective mates and establish a hierarchy. Both genders remain sexually active until late August or September.

Cottontail does are polyestrous, accepting numerous mates and birthing as many as four litters per season. There is no bond, and mates go their separate ways after breeding; this promiscuity ensures a varied gene pool. Prior to mating, cottontails perform a courtship ritual in which the buck chases a doe until she tires and turns to face him. The pair rises on hind legs and spars briefly with the forepaws, then both drop to all fours, nose to nose, and the male jumps straight upward to a height of about two feet. The female replies by jumping upward, too, and both may repeat the action several times. This jumping behavior probably demonstrates the fitness of either animal to mate.

Once pregnant, does spurn further sexual advances. Gestation lasts thirty days, at the end of which expectant mothers retire to a sheltered burrow. There, in a grass-lined nest that has been insulated with fur nipped from the mother's underbelly and from around her four pairs of nipples, she births as many as eight naked and blind (altricial) young. Newborns weigh just 25 to 35 grams but grow fast, gaining more than 2 grams per day, and by five days they have opened their eyes.

By two weeks, young cottontails are fully furred and venture outside the burrow to feed on vegetation. At this point the mother is nursing them only twice a day and may already be pregnant with her next litter. Weaning occurs at twenty days, and the young rabbits, suddenly intolerant of one another, disperse.

Behaviorisms

While not a long-distance runner, an adult cottontail can exceed 18 miles per hour through thick brush, leaping 12 feet and instantly changing direction. A flaw that human hunters exploit is that rabbits tend to run in a circle when pursued, coming back to cross their own trails and thereby confusing the noses of animal predators. Human hunters have learned to take advantage of this by using dogs to chase rabbits back to where they stand. Being a sprinter with poor long-distance vision, a startled cottontail will often flee to a nearby bush and freeze. Many a cottontail has fallen to .22 rifles in this manner, because human vision is sharper than a rabbit's. Cottontails are also staples of the fur trade, although their silky pelts are made less desirable if the thin skin is torn. Uses include trimming boot tops, parka hoods, and mittens, and sometimes pelts make an entire fur coat. Rabbit fur isn't waterproof or rugged, but it is plentiful, inexpensive, and nice to touch, and a market exists for plews (prime skins).

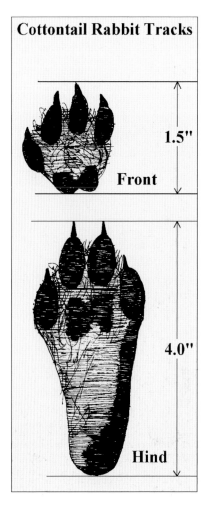

Cottontails are not well liked by farmers, gardeners, or landscapers. Their summer feeding and reproductive capacity can mean tremendous damage to crops, while winter browsing of shrubs and fruit trees makes them pests on golf courses and in orchards. The problem is exacerbated by a human reluctance to permit the cottontail's natural predators to live near homes.

Except for brief encounters during the summer mating season, eastern cottontails are solitary and intolerant of one another. Territorial sizes are dependent on food and other resources but generally encompass between five and eight acres. Male territories tend to overlap or include the territories of local does.

Every predator considers the cottontail prey. Hawks, owls, and eagles hunt them from the air; skunks and other weasels prey on the young; bobcats pounce on them; and coyotes chase them through the underbrush. The rabbit's best defense is to sprint out of sight along a maze of trails and scents that can confuse the keenest nose. Most cottontails won't survive into their third year, but reproductive rates are high enough to ensure that this species is unlikely to be threatened by hunting or predation.

About the Author

Len McDougall is a professional outdoorsman with four decades of sometimes hard experience in the north woods. Len is an internationally recognized survival instructor/tracker, and author of the books, *The Encyclopedia of Tracks & Scats, The Log Cabin: An Adventure, Practical Outdoor Survival, Practical Outdoor Projects, The Complete Tracker, The Outdoors Almanac, The Snowshoe Handbook, The Field & Stream Wilderness Survival Handbook* and *Made for the Outdoors*. He teaches survival, snowshoeing, kayaking, dogsledding, and tracking classes, and works as a wilderness guide.

Len's interest in all things natural began early. Having grown up with youngsters of the Odawa and Ojibwa tribes in Northern Michigan, the Elders considered him more Nish-na-bee (Indian) than Chee-mook-a-mon (white), and accepted the Scots-Irish kid as one of their own. With that status, he received the teachings of the Grandfathers, who are obligated by culture to pass what they know to the next generation. With no written language the tribes had already lost much, but what remained was enough to strike young Len's heart with a passion that would subsequently consume his life.

At twelve Len was backpacking solo for a week at a time in summer. At thirteen he was running a trapline to provide his family with meat and with money from the sale of pelts. At sixteen, he nearly died of hypothermia during his first solo winter camping trip when an unpredicted blizzard buried his camp. The following summer he was bitten by a Massasauga rattlesnake and survived three days alone in the woods before finding his way back home ("Snakebitten!," *Michigan Out-of-Doors*, October '85/ *Woods-N-Water News*, July '04). At twenty-three, he was given up for dead by local authorities while backpacking in -35 degree windchills. At twenty-seven, he was again given up for dead under similar conditions. At thirty-eight, he was stranded for three days alone in a blizzard with windchills that exceeded -65 degrees, but no one considered him to be in danger. At age forty-five, he built a log cabin homestead, with hand-dug well, using only hand tools, "just to see what the old-timers went through" (*The Log Cabin: An Adventure*, Globe Pequot Press, June '03).

In March 1997, Len discovered the first pair of mating timber wolves to migrate south to Michigan's Lower Peninsula in 100 years. For the next five years, he guided biologists from the Natural Resources Commission of the Little Traverse Bay Band of Odawa Indians into local wolf habitats to gather data on what has now become a thriving population. Len also served as Team Tracker for the Northern Michigan Wolf Detection and Habitat Survey Team.

Having forged a career in Manufacturing Quality Control for ten years prior to becoming a writer, Len has found a niche in evaluating and writing about outdoor products. He has evaluated products for more than 150 manufacturers, including Coleman, Vasque, Winchester, Current Designs, Pelican International, Atlas Snowshoes, La Crosse, Kelty, MSR, Jansport, Kodak, Pentax, Nikon, Slumberjack, Tasco, Timex, Simmons, Buck Knives, Brunton, and Remington. His real-life, long-term field tests find flaws that were not apparent in less rigorous trials, and his findings have been used numerous times to improve existing products. He has been called on to evaluate conceptual designs and prototypes before they reach the marketplace, and Consumers Digest has hired him to award its coveted Best Buy rating to more than twenty outdoor products.

Born in 1956, Len says he's had more financially lucrative jobs than working in and writing about the great out-of-doors, but none have been more fulfilling. He likes to think that what he writes is a contribution to the well-being of fellow outdoorsman, and he openly admits to being an idealistic fool who's out to change the world into a better, nicer place for tomorrow's generations.

A grandfather himself, Len has assumed the obligation to pass along what he learned from his Indian mentors. He smiles without humor at the recent trend toward being "green." "I've always known that if Hollywood said it was cool to be an environmentalist, everyone would be one." Although considered a loner by the people who know him, Len prides himself on lending a helping hand to those in need. In his own words, "There are only two rules to a good life: Always do the right thing, and always be the Good Guy. Everything else will follow."